What's a Teen to Do?

What's a Teen to Do?

Developing Helping Skills
With 14- to 16-Year-Olds

John A. Flanagan

Nihil Obstat: Rev. Nicholas Lohkamp, O.F.M.
　　　　　　　　Rev. Robert L. Hagedorn

Imprimi Potest: Rev. Jeremy Harrington, O.F.M.
　　　　　　　　　Provincial

Imprimatur: +James H. Garland, V.G.
　　　　　　　Archdiocese of Cincinnati
　　　　　　　May 19, 1989

The *nihil obstat* and *imprimatur* are a declaration that a book is considered to be free from doctrinal or moral error. It is not implied that those who have granted the *nihil obstat* and *imprimatur* agree with the contents, opinions or statements expressed.

Cover and book design by Julie Lonneman

ISBN 0-86716-119-1

Published by St. Anthony Messenger Press
Printed in the U.S.A.

Contents

Stories for Would-Be Helpers

"I couldn't sleep—not right away. I was too excited. I helped someone! It made me feel great! I know he's better because I helped. I know I'm better because I helped. Now I can't wait for a chance to help someone else."

That's what a 14-year-old told me when I was a part-time teacher and coach in a boys' orphanage. With the help of some fantastic nuns, he had discovered the satisfaction of helping others.

The stories and discussion questions in this book will help parents, religious educators, teachers and youth ministers lead 14- to 16-year-olds to the same discovery. It will build helping skills and encourage teens to discover both the joy of helping and the relief of being helped.

Why 14- to 16-year-olds? Young people of this age exhibit two flourishing traits: (1) They are rapidly becoming free from adult supervision of their decisions. (2) The importance of their peer group is mushrooming. Greater freedom and greater reliance on one another increase both opportunities to help and situational invitations to help. The same factors increase reliance on one's peers; accepting help from peers is a natural consequence.

While helping and helpful attitudes may not be the most influential factors in establishing positive peer relationships, they are certainly of major importance. Helpful attitudes should be fostered early in adolescence so that these attitudes may grow as the youngster grows. Developing helping skills is another step in the process of growing up.

The Christian outlook certainly supports helpfulness. In Matthew's Last Judgment scene, Jesus says: "Amen, I say to you, whatever you did for one of these least brothers of mine, you did for me" (Matthew 25:41). Jesus also offered the Good Samaritan to illustrate the second half of the Great Commandment: "You

1

shall love your neighbor as yourself" (see Luke 10:25-37).

How to Use This Book

These stories are designed to invite discussion among adults and young teens at home, in the classroom or in the youth group. In the home they provide material for a dinner-table exchange, a family evening discussion or a one-on-one talk between parent and teen. In the classroom or a youth group the stories can be used for large- or small-group discussion; a teacher may use them for a creative writing exercise. In any setting they can be used to help teens think through a real-life situation which has arisen. (The issues are identified parenthetically in the Table of Contents.)

The stories in this book fall into four classifications. All of them present situations in which a youngster may help another, but each section focuses on a different helping skill.

The purpose of Part One, "Noticing Needs," is to sensitize young people to opportunities for helping. Cries for help take many forms, both verbal and nonverbal. A cry for help may be acted out clearly or subtly; it may be spoken in loud, clear words. A helping person must first learn to recognize a cry for help in all its variety. The stories in this section present teens at the moment of discerning another's need for aid and ask teens to help define the need.

In Part Two, "Shaping Strategies," the reader enters into a dialogue with the teen narrator of the stories. These stories invite an empathetic response—developing helping strategies which consider not only the need but also the personalities involved. Empathy, the ability to put oneself into another's shoes, is a critical factor in helping relationships. We must understand the position of the person to be helped in order to do a really effective job of helping. In this section the stories present youngsters trying to decide how to help another and invite teens to enter into that decision process.

Part Three, "Evaluating Efforts," is also in dialogue form. It asks teens to decide whether or not a would-be helper has made a positive impact. True helpfulness is neither taking full responsibility for meeting another's needs nor making the other bear total responsibility for fulfilling his or her own need. A healthy helping attitude falls somewhere in between. A good helper provides new concepts of choice while respecting the other as a unique individual created by God. Such respect leaves the recipient free to assume final responsibility, for true helping is never manipulative. The stories here depict teens involved in helping efforts and invite criticism of their efforts.

Part Four, "Taking Time," encourages patience. Few helping efforts bring instant results. More often, a helper is involved over a period of time. The recipient's progress with a problem may seem discouragingly slow; indeed, often we never know whether or not our offering was helpful. The stories in this section present lengthier involvement in helping situations and ask teens to judge the worth of further efforts.

The process for using this book can be adapted to different settings. First ask the teens to read a story—silently or aloud, in a group or in private—and allow some time for reflection on the fictional situation. Use the questions which follow the story to begin the discussion. Avoid judging or rejecting an answer; an accepting climate is essential to fruitful discussion. Just try to elicit the *reasons* underlying the conclusion. Remember that the object is not to find the "right" answer (there isn't one), but to help a young person make conscious helping decisions.

Some Assumptions

The questions attached to each story are raised in the context of certain assumptions about the nature of helping. Parents, religious educators, teachers and youth leaders should keep these assumptions in mind as the discussion proceeds.

1) *We create the "chance" to help.* Opportunities to help rarely drop from the sky. More often we slowly develop awareness of another's need. That awareness marks the time of decision. We may choose not to help—and not necessarily because we lack charity. The refusal to help may be an exercise of prudence. After all, only God is equipped to be a helper in each and every situation. Once a negative decision is made, we probably will not pass that way again.

2) *We can help too much*. When we set out to help someone, the objective must be to help them help themselves, not to become a crutch. Young people need to evaluate situations where too much or too little help was given in order to gain the ability to discern the mean. Many such examples can be provided by youth themselves: "If I ask your help with a math problem, and you do it for me, then I need you again for the next problem. If you lead me to the solution but make me do the work, there is a good chance I can do the next problem by myself."

3) *We can sometimes help by doing almost nothing*. Often the best help is just being there. For instance, when a teenage girl's puppy was killed by a car, two friends came to her aid. They helped her wrap and bury the furry body; one of them transplanted a clump of flowers from his own yard over the grave. With simple gestures and few words, they gave great comfort.

4) *Our experience helps us decide what is helpful*. Adults and teens alike can profit from sharing their experiences of needing and receiving help. Experience is the first way we become familiar with the dynamics of helping and a key basis for evaluating other helping efforts.

5) *We find some people hard to help*. Some people really are hard to help; they refuse all offers. Others we find difficult to approach because we perceive them as somehow "different" because their race or ethnic group, looks (good or bad!), personality, physical or mental abilities are markedly different from our own. A necessary strategy is to keep in mind that all kinds of people are receptive to a caring approach.

6) *Some needs are more than we can handle*. Adults should be frank about knowing the limits of one's ability to help. There are times when all of us must turn to the professionals; there are certainly times when a youth should seek advice from a trusted adult.

7) *Sometimes it is right to refuse to help*. Whenever we find our own integrity threatened by a person or a situation, it's time to say no. Being able to recognize when our own morality is at risk is a criterion for being a good helper.

8) *We may not always succeed in our efforts*. This is the most painful reality of helping interactions. We may have little impact on what we see as the needs of the person we are trying to help.

Perhaps we have misdefined the need; perhaps the other person simply refuses our help. Or perhaps we really have helped in ways we cannot see or guess.

9) *A helping attitude is "caught" as well as taught.* A last word to adults who work with youth: Modeling is of frontline importance. Helpful adults generate helpful young people through imitation. Helpfulness, because it satisfies needs in us all, attracts both young and old to the role of helper.

PART ONE

Noticing Needs

We begin a helpful response by deciding what the other person needs. Then we can plan some strategy to fulfill those needs.

The stories in this section present teens discovering other people's problems and acquaint young people with the variety of opportunities for helping. In all our lives, the options to help are unlimited. Young people need to learn to recognize needs before they can decide what is helpful.

The stories in this section are designed to help teens consider the following points:

- how the helper recognized the need to be helpful;

- whether or not the person being helped realized that he or she *needed* help;

- whether or not the person being helped realized he or she *had been* helped;

- whether or not what the helper *decided* was really helpful;

- whether or not what the helper *did* was really helpful;

- what else the helper might have done.

The Tutor

On his first day in tenth grade, Scott sat watching other students enter the classroom. Many of them were classmates from junior high. Others he knew from community activities.

One exception sat very still in the front row. As Scott learned when the students had to introduce themselves, Dolores Sandoval was from Venezuela. She spoke no English. Mrs. Reid explained to the class that Dolores would be taking intensive English and that she would certainly appreciate help from anyone.

When the bell signaled the end of class, Scott walked up to Dolores. He smiled and began speaking in faltering Spanish. Dolores smiled and her dark eyes sparkled brightly. She began to speak Spanish excitedly and very rapidly.

"Wait! Wait!" Scott said in English, holding up his hands as he spoke.

Dolores stopped talking.

"Look, *hablo pocito Español*, I speak Spanish only a little," Scott explained. "I will help you with English if I can."

Dolores was staying with her great-uncle, her grandfather's brother, just three blocks past Scott's home. Scott managed to walk her home after school. As they went along, Scott stopped and pointed to objects, saying the English word for each.

Scott and Dolores made an agreement. She would try to speak to him in English. He would speak to her in Spanish. When he taught her a new word, she taught him the Spanish equivalent. Each day Dolores learned more English—from Scott, from other students at school and especially from intensive English. And Scott was learning more Spanish than his classes had ever given him.

"Don't students study English in Venezuela?" he asked her.

"Not in San Carlos. The population is small and it is deep in southern Venezuela—on the border with Colombia, not far from Brazil."

For the first six weeks of school, Scott and Dolores walked to and from school together. She was increasingly able to participate in her classes. She made many friends as she conversed with classmates. Scott felt proud of his pupil and of himself, even though he endured daily episodes of teasing for walking her home.

One afternoon Dolores faced Scott, a serious look on her face. "Barry wants to buy me an ice cream sundae," she told him. "Is it all right if I don't walk home with you today?"

He felt the anger rise within him. The question was totally unexpected and he had trouble finding an answer. A simple OK would do, but it took him a minute to get it out.

She hurried away, leaving him agitated and lonely. He was angry and he didn't understand why.

Noticing Needs

1) In what ways did Scott try to help Dolores? What did it cost him?

2) Did Scott gain anything by helping? What did he gain?

3) What might have motivated Scott to help Dolores? Of his possible motives, which do you think were most worthy; which least worthy?

4) Why did Scott become angry when Dolores asked about the sundae?

Putting Yourself in the Story

If you were Scott, what would you do next?

Crossing the Delaware

Krysten was a beautiful girl who sat like a statue in the classroom, tense and silent in the front row. She rarely interacted with anyone. When someone talked to her alone, her extreme shyness bordered on tense fear. As a result, she had no friends. "She is so pretty but so strange," other students would say.

Krysten barely passed first semester of sophomore history. Then one day a new student enrolled. He was tall, muscular and black. He was glib, with a delightful sense of humor. He was assigned the desk next to Krysten. Mrs. Foster, the history teacher, asked him to introduce himself. He stood and faced the class.

"My name is Hamilton Jones," he began, displaying gleaming white teeth that contrasted with his black skin. "Everybody calls me Ham cause that's the way I am!" Ham laughed and everyone joined him in a round of giggles.

"I'm good with names. By tomorrow, I'll know you all. I already know her name. She's Mrs. Foster," he said, pointing to the teacher and grinning.

Ham and Krysten were a striking portrait of total difference. She was petite; he was large. Her skin glowed like white marble; his gleamed black. She sat in almost total silence while he was already whispering to the others around him. She had sat there for a long time without participating; in his first hour, he was volunteering information and comments.

When the bell rang, he turned to her. "You're Krysten, aren't you?" he asked.

She swallowed hard and nodded yes. He didn't embarrass her. Instead, he jumped to his feet. "See you tomorrow, neighbor," he laughed and was gone.

The next day, a new assignment made Krysten shudder. "You are going to prepare dialogue reports," Mrs. Foster explained. "Each of you must choose a partner. Each pair will then pick some incident in American history. Then you will report the incident to the class by talking to each other. Plan an outline of your dialogue and be ready to present your report a week from tomorrow."

During the next several classes, Mrs. Foster stood at her desk taking down the names of partners for the reports. "Hamilton, do you have a partner?" she asked one day.

"No, but I'd like Krysten," Ham answered. Then he asked, "Does the report have to come from what we're studying now?"

"This report can be on anything in American history," Mrs. Foster explained.

Ham turned to Krysten. "That makes it easy," he laughed. "How about Washington crossing the Delaware? Do you want to do that?"

"I guess so," Krysten replied.

Ham ignored the girl's timidity and forced her to work with him. When the day came to present their report, Ham brought a pair of oars and a sawhorse on which he had mounted oarlocks. Krysten was Washington, standing on a chair in front of the sawhorse; Ham was the crew, sitting on the sawhorse and rowing.

"It's bitter cold up here," Krysten said, her voice trembling.

"I know, George, but we gotta surprise them Hessians!" the oarsman reminded Washington.

Over and over again, Krysten repeated her one line. Each reply from Ham added more information to the report. He kept rowing and his humor kept the class laughing. Before the report was completed, Krysten astonished everyone. She began to laugh along with everyone else. Someone began to clap, and soon the whole class was clapping. There were two lines left in the report, but Ham dropped his oars and extended his hand to help Krysten step down. She was smiling.

Noticing Needs

1) Should her classmates try to help Krysten become less "strange?" Why or why not?

2) Do you think her classmates wanted to help Krysten? Why?

3) How does Ham go about helping Krysten?

4) Do we have a responsibility to help a girl like Krysten? Why or why not?

5) Describe some other ways to help Krysten.

Putting Yourself in the Story

If you were Ham, what would you do next?

An Unhappy Friend

Erin slumped lazily in the chair in Debbie's room. She had said nothing for several minutes. Debbie sat on the bed carefully pushing a needle in and out of her cross-stitch.

"Debbie, I feel *awful*," Erin said abruptly.

Debbie laid her work on the bed and turned to face her friend. "What's wrong?" she asked.

"Last night I stayed awake listening to my mom and dad. Mom said she won't have a divorce. Dad said that it didn't matter—that he's leaving."

"Wow! He must have been really mad," observed Debbie.

"Yeah, I guess both of them are," Erin agreed. "They're always fighting. I don't know if my little brother knows how bad it is, but I've heard them a lot of nights."

"Don't you think they'll make up?"

Erin considered Debbie's question. "No," she said, "they've done that before, but this time I think Dad means it. He's leaving."

Debbie stared silently. "No wonder you've been acting goofy lately," she commented.

Erin frowned. "What do you mean, goofy?"

"Well, not goofy," Debbie corrected. "Just different. You pout. You don't pay attention anymore. You get mad. And you're always griping about having a stomachache."

"Really? I didn't know I was like that," said Erin. "I just can't stop worrying."

On their way to school a few days later Erin told Debbie that her father had left. Debbie could hear the hurt in her friend's voice. She didn't know what to say. She just stayed close to Erin during the day. Last period they had English together. Their teacher assigned a project: Each student was to build a model showing a scene from the play they were reading. "Your dad can help you," the teacher said.

"What a rotten thing for her to say," Erin remarked as they walked home.

A few days later the physical education class started playing softball. The teacher, Ms. Foley, stopped Erin after class. "You need some throwing and catching practice," she said. "Can your mother play catch?"

"No," Erin answered.

"You have a little brother, don't you? Play catch with him. You'll both learn."

Ms. Foley gave Erin a pat on the shoulder, smiled and walked on.

"At least she didn't say my dad," Erin commented to Debbie.

Over the next few days, Debbie realized that when she talked about her own dad, Erin's eyes filled with tears.

Noticing Needs

1) Should Debbie attempt to help Erin handle her unhappiness? If so, what can she do?

2) Since divorce is a family affair, should Debbie stay out of it completely?

3) Could Debbie become a "crutch" for Erin? How can Debbie avoid doing this?

4) Should Debbie approach others to help Erin? Whom should she approach and what should she say?

5) Are there any actions Debbie should not take? What are they?

Putting Yourself in the Story

If you were Debbie, what would you do?

Too Many Schools

When Gilberto and his parents moved into the little stucco house next door to Chris, the two boys became friends immediately. Chris learned that Gil's father had been a migrant worker for many years, that his mother had died a year ago and that his father had recently remarried.

"You can probably take the same ninth-grade classes I do," suggested Chris.

"I have many problems in school," Gil informed him.

"What do you mean?" asked Chris.

"I can't read or write very well. Most of my teachers felt sorry for me; they just passed me every year. You know, in eight years I've been in 21 schools."

"Wow!" remarked Chris.

"I was the oldest boy, so I worked the fields with my father. That way I missed a lot of school," said Gil. After a pause, he continued. "My dad has a regular job now. Here it is June. It seems strange not to be working in the fields," Gil reported.

Chris nodded. "Listen, if you want to I can help with reading and writing," he suggested to Gil.

Gil beamed. "That'd be great," he said.

Almost every day of the summer they read together from books and comics and papers. Gil practiced writing by copying pages from magazines. Gil improved, but not enough. They reported to the junior high where they both entered the ninth grade. During the first week of school, Gil went to their history teacher, Mr. Anderson.

"I know we will have to read a lot for your class," he said. "I will need some help to learn to read."

"That's not my responsibility," Mr. Anderson answered.

Gil went to his father. "I know you want me to have a good education. I need to learn to read."

"You already learned that in the other schools," his father replied. "Now you study!"

When Gil told Chris about Mr. Anderson and his father, Chris talked to their English teacher. Mrs. Martin scheduled 45 minutes before school each day to work with Gil.

At lunch Chris told his friend Peggy all about Gil. "I wish we could all help him," Chris said. "He's really smart. He could get all A's if he could read and write better."

Noticing Needs

1) Should Gil's peers try to help him? What can they do?

2) How might Gil feel about getting help from his peers?

3) How has Chris tried to help Gil? Are his efforts appropriate?

4) What do you think of Mr. Anderson's response to Gil's request?

5) Do you think it was a good idea for Chris to talk to the English teacher?

6) What is the value of learning to read in the ninth grade? What are some of the difficulties?

Putting Yourself in the Story

If you were Chris, what would you do next?

A Room to Live In

For years Angie, Louise, Jenny, Anne and Gail had been best friends. If one was involved in a school activity, the others would probably be there with her. But Gail never invited any of them home.

Then Gail's parents got a divorce. It was an angry separation. Gail was given the choice of which parent she wanted to live with. She was not too happy with either of them, but living with her mother meant she could be with her friends. So that was her choice.

Her friends all came from happy home situations. Gail tried to explain what her home life was like: "My father is an alcoholic, but it's not any easier living without him. My mother has more boyfriends than I can count. They come day and night. That's the reason that I never ask any of you to stay over."

Her friends offered expressions of sympathy and asked if there was some way for them to help her. She told them probably nothing could be done. She had a room to live in even if her mom's behavior made her life at home miserable.

"That's why I can't wait until I can support myself," Gail told them. "That's why I'm taking all I can on microcomputers. I'm already very good at word processing."

Later, when Gail was not with them, her friends searched for ways they might help her. "Gail is so smart," Angie began. "She always makes the honor roll, but I'm afraid she'll be quitting school soon."

"Yeah, I know," added Louise. "I wish she'd stay and try for some scholarship. She ought to go to college."

Jenny broke in: "She has so many problems. I just wish we could help her."

"If we work at it," Anne suggested, "maybe we can find a way."

Angie shook her head. "I already asked mom if she could live with us," she reported. "Mom just said that Gail has a mother. She doesn't think we'd be helping Gail by hurting her mother."

They were even more concerned the next time Gail was with them. "I've been thinking about running away," Gail explained.

"I won't, though, because that way I'd lose you guys, too."

The girls kept striving to find an answer to the problem.

Louise suggested, "We need to go to someone. We can't do much by ourselves."

"I thought of that, too," Jenny reported. "I talked to the school counselor and he said if Gail isn't being abused, the school can't do anything. I talked to our pastor and he promised to stop and ask Gail and her mother to attend church. I'm not sure what that will bring."

"What if we talk to our moms in a group?" Anne proposed. "All four of us can talk to each mom."

They decided to try Anne's suggestion. Her mom was first. After hearing their whole story, she had a question of her own.

"Have you talked to Gail's mom?" she asked.

"No, we can't do that," the girls chorused.

"Okay, I'm glad," Anne's mother agreed. "I have just one idea. Maybe, after you talk to the other mothers, you can figure a way to invite Gail to stay with each of you fairly often. That would give her some time away from her mother. And it would give each of you a special time to convince her to stay in school."

Noticing Needs

1) Is it helpful to provide Gail with an "escape" a few days each week? Explain.

2) Was Angie being helpful when she asked her mom if Gail could live with Angie's family? Was her mom being helpful when she said no? Why or why not?

3) Is it really helpful for the girls to attempt to do anything about Gail's home situation? Why or why not?

4) Is it a good move for the girls to talk to each of their four mothers? Why?

5) Is it helpful to encourage Gail to stay in school? Why?

Putting Yourself in the Story

If you were one of Gail's close friends, how would you help her?

Connie's Concern

"I get so angry when I'm babysitting my little brothers and sisters," Connie declared. "I'm afraid of myself."

Lara stared at her friend. The intensity of Connie's statement surprised her. They had been friends for several years, but this was not the Connie Lara knew. "What do you mean?"

"Oh, I read a lot about child abuse," Connie replied. "Sometimes I think I'm gonna slug one of the kids—even the baby."

Lara was still perplexed. "I don't believe you'd do that," she protested.

"Don't be too sure," Connie cautioned.

Lara couldn't think of anything to say. She sorted the books and papers on her desk into three neat piles, while Connie remained propped against the pillows on Lara's bed. It was several minutes before either of them spoke.

"Do you sit them a lot?" Lara inquired.

"I will from now on. Dad is always on the road during the week, and now Mom is going to work part-time. She's going to leave the house and the kids to me every day."

"Every day?" Lara asked. "I thought you said part-time."

"Five days a week—every evening from six till nine-thirty," Connie explained.

"But what makes you think you'll get mad at the kids?" Lara asked.

"They always get to me. Just little things—Jimmy is whiny; Bobby is sassy. Sue is always into things and the baby spits up a lot."

"Have you talked to your mom about the way you feel?"

Connie shook her head. "No, I won't do that. She's so excited about this job. She says she is going to save what she makes for an extra-special family vacation. Besides—" Connie turned and buried her head in the pillow.

"Besides, what?" Lara pressed.

"Nothing."

Lara, puzzled, stared at the back of her friend's head. Suddenly Connie lifted her head. "If I tell you something, will you promise never to tell?"

Lara considered the question for just a moment. "I'll never tell anyone," she promised.

"I think my mom wants to go to work because she has the same problem with the kids I do."

Noticing Needs

1) Should Connie be anxious about her feelings? Why or why not?

2) Do you think there is any danger if Connie keeps on babysitting? Why or why not?

3) Can Lara help Connie? How?

4) Should Lara encourage Connie to talk to a trusted adult? Why or why not?

5) Should Lara convince Connie to talk to her mom? Why or why not?

Putting Yourself in the Story

If you were Lara, what would you do?

On the Bench

Jared grabbed his sweater out of the rented truck and pulled it on. The mild day was turning cold. He shivered a bit as he continued to carry cartons from the truck. They were almost moved into the small house his father had bought. The ground around the house was level and the soil looked very fertile. Jared thought he'd like it here.

The following Monday he enrolled at the high school. He quickly saw that he was the only black student there. As he went from one class to another almost no one talked to him. One student, a big guy named Nolan, was in all his morning classes. Nolan seemed friendly; he talked for a while each time they met. At lunch Jared and Nolan sat at a table together. No one joined them.

"Is this an unfriendly place?" Jared asked.

Nolan smiled at him. "This little town has never seen a black person. I guess they don't know how to take you."

"Then why are you different?" inquired Jared.

Nolan's smile widened. "My dad's a consulting engineer. He took us with him to Africa a couple years ago. We were the only whites in town."

Jared grinned his appreciation.

"Hey, you're the right size and shape to be a basketball player. Do you play?" Nolan asked.

"Sure do," Jared replied. "I love it."

"Then come out for the team. We started last week."

After school, Jared went with Nolan to meet the coach. A little later, he was on the floor with the team. When players saw him jump above everyone for rebounds, most of them accepted him.

Three games into the season, Jared had not played a minute. He suited up and sat on the bench. Nolan approached the coach. "Coach, why aren't you playing Jared?"

"I call that question out of line," the coach snapped. "I play my best five. That's it!"

"Okay, coach," Nolan said quietly. "But Jared's better than I am so maybe I should sit on the bench with him."

"I can arrange that," the coach growled. His face had turned a deep red.

After Jared and Nolan had sat side by side through the next game, Nolan's father came to his son's room to talk. They sat together on the side of the bed.

"Why did you get benched?" his father asked. When Nolan explained, his dad smiled. "Is Jared that good?"

"Dad, he's better than anyone who ever played here—much better."

"Do you want me to get involved?" his father asked.

"No. Not yet anyway."

The older man smiled, slapped Nolan on the shoulder and left.

Noticing Needs

1) What is the nature and the extent of Jared's problem?

2) How does Nolan attempt to help Jared?

3) Nolan's effort to help Jared with the coach cost him his own chance to play. Is that smart? Why or why not?

4) What difficulties does Nolan face in trying to help Jared? What should Nolan try?

5) Should Nolan ask his father to "get involved?" Why or why not?

Putting Yourself in the Story

If you were Nolan, what would you do?

'No Dogs!'

Ruth and Heidi were laughing together as they neared the library. Engrossed in their conversation, they failed to see the large German shepherd come charging across a yard until he barked sharply. He stood only inches away, growling at them.

Ruth gasped for breath as she stood frozen in fear. Heidi started in surprise but recovered almost immediately. On one side of her Ruth trembled in terror; on her other side the big dog trembled as he growled. Slowly, Heidi held out a book toward the dog.

"Stay, big guy," she said firmly. The animal still snarled.

"No!" Heidi snapped. "Stay. Stay." She held the book a little closer. The dog stopped snarling and sniffed the book.

"Good boy!" Heidi said quietly. The dog took a step toward her and sniffed her hand. She kept talking quietly. He rubbed his head against her hand. She shifted the book carefully to her other hand and gently touched his neck. He wagged his tail and she began to pet him. He stood panting, his tail switching back and forth.

"You wanta meet him?" Heidi asked Ruth.

Ruth could hardly talk; her eyes were filled with tears. Still trembling, she answered, "He's terrible! I don't want him close to me. Send him away!"

Heidi ruffled the fur on the back of the dog's neck. He raised his head toward her. She pointed to the house. "Go, boy," she ordered. The animal turned slowly away, then ran to the house.

Later, back at Heidi's home, Ruth talked with her friend. "My Uncle Joe breeds golden retrievers," she told Heidi. "He wants to give me a pup out of the next litter. I don't want it. I'm afraid of dogs."

"Yeah, I can see that. But retrievers are gentle. You'll like a puppy," Heidi assured her.

"My uncle says that, too. But he's not afraid of dogs!"

"Yeah. He and my dad take their dogs to a lot of the same shows," said Heidi. She paused. "Listen, why don't you come outside and see our puppies," she invited.

Ruth refused at first, but finally she agreed. Out in the yard near their pen, Heidi sat on the grass with six little Siberian huskies climbing all over her. She cuddled them, rolled them on the ground and scratched their ears. Ruth stood well off to the side, unable to come close.

After a few minutes, Heidi put all but one puppy back in the pen. She called Ruth over to get acquainted. The furry little animal came to each of them, begging for attention. He was soft and wiggled at every touch. Ruth finally held him, but as she did, he chose to chew on her hand. She pushed him toward Heidi.

"Put him away!" she said.

Noticing Needs

1) Should Heidi try to help Ruth overcome her fear? If so, what should she do?

2) Are there precautions that Heidi should observe?

3) Is it possible to help someone overcome very deep fears?

4) If Ruth continues to insist she never wants to be near a dog, should Heidi forget helping her?

5) Could Heidi find someone else to help Ruth? Who? What might that person do?

Putting Yourself in the Story

If you were Heidi, what would you do?

'Not Me!'

Todd and Brian had been friends for a long time. They lived only two blocks apart. They had started school together, been on the same Little League teams, shared scouting experiences. Both were 16 and sophomores in high school.

It was almost a year and a half ago that Todd first offered Brian some whiskey. Todd had taken a bottle from the nightclub his father owned. The business was very successful—Todd's parents worked long hours to make it so. That left Todd at home alone much of the time.

"Here, try it," Todd suggested, holding the bottle toward Brian.

"Nope," Brian said simply.

"Oh, come on," Todd urged.

"Not me," Brian replied firmly. "I had an uncle who died because he couldn't leave that stuff alone. Not me!"

The argument went on. Not every visit Brian made to his friend's home brought an invitation to drink liquor, but it happened often until the night Brian made his declaration.

"The next time you bug me with that stuff, I quit coming to see you," he informed his friend. "I said no every time. I mean no. Don't push it at me."

Todd did stop inviting Brian to join him, but he did not stop drinking. Brian knew this and it bothered him. He was angry with Todd for stealing the liquor from his father. He told Todd that just having a bottle was illegal, since they were both minors. His arguments did not impress Todd in the least. Brian thought about not going over to Todd's anymore, but he just couldn't betray their close friendship. He considered telling Todd's parents what he knew, but ratting on his friend seemed worse. The whole thing became more confusing every day.

Then one night as they watched TV in Todd's living room, his friend turned to Brian. "Do you think I might be an alcoholic?" he asked in an almost beseeching tone.

Brian felt a little shudder inside. He ducked the question. "Why ask me? I'm no expert."

Todd frowned. "You're my friend. You must know."

"What makes you ask?" Brian inquired.

"I'm taking more of my dad's booze," he said. "I'm scared I'm gonna get caught but I want more. So I do it more often—take the stuff, I mean. I hide out here and drink alone. I knock myself out lots of nights."

"What do you mean?" asked Brian.

"Oh, I take enough to get a buzz. Then I go to bed and sleep it off. I say I'll quit when I want to. Am I an alcoholic?" Todd asked in the same pleading way.

"Maybe yes. Maybe no. I really don't know. I do think you're working on becoming one," Brian answered.

Noticing Needs

1) Can Brian help Todd? If so, what should he do?

2) Is it really possible to do anything to help Todd?

3) Are there family implications to helping Todd?

4) Are there legal implications to helping Todd?

5) Are there times when it's best to protect yourself?

Putting Yourself in the Story

If you were Brian, what would you do?

Sudden Good-bye

Rod and Ross were twins. Rod and Sheila had recently agreed to go steady, but Sheila complained jokingly that she never knew which twin was with her. Among the things that Sheila loved to do was to ride horses. Rod disliked horses; Ross rode a lot. When they talked about horses, Sheila could tell the twins apart.

Early in May, Sheila came up with a great idea. "Hey, let's have a riding party," she suggested. "We can rent horses at Covered Wagon Stables. How about Saturday?"

Her excitement spread to several other students. Before long, 12 students planned together for the riding party. Rod agreed even though he was the least enthusiastic of them all. On Saturday, they rode their bikes out to the stables and picked up their horses. Mr. Carney, one of the physical education teachers, had accepted their invitation to ride with them.

A cowboy from the stables led them out onto an easy trail that wound through low hills with numerous outcroppings of rock. Mr. Carney brought up the rear. From time to time the trail ran at the base of low cliffs. On the slopes above were deposits of loose gravel-like rock. At one of these spots the loose rock began to give way, creating a small slide of sand and small stones. As the slide came down in front of Sheila's horse, the animal reared to avoid the stones. Then he whirled away from the spot, stepping in a hole as he did. Sheila tumbled from the saddle head first, striking her head on a large boulder. The horse fell on top of her.

Ross alertly jumped from his mount, grabbed the bridle of Sheila's horse and helped the animal to its feet. A little slap on the rump moved the horse out of the way. Ross knelt beside Sheila and called her name. There was no answer. Her hair was already filled with blood from the head wound. She lay there, her body twisted from the fall of the horse. Ross raised his head, his eyes moist and his face ashen.

"Rod," he said softly. "I think she's dead."

Mr. Carney knelt beside Sheila to administer CPR. Rod moaned something under his breath, then turned and ran to the cowboy.

"Hurry and get an ambulance in here!" he ordered.

The man spurred his horse back along the trail toward the stables. Sheila still had not moved when he returned an hour later with two Jeeps and paramedics from the sheriff's rescue team. They examined Sheila and covered her sadly.

After Sheila's death, Rod refused to go back to school. Hugh, Rod's closest friend after Ross, tried to encourage him to come back to school. So did Emily and Paula, Sheila's closest friends.

The night following the funeral, Rod asked Ross to go walking with him. They had walked in silence through the darkness for an hour before Rod spoke. "We can go home now," he said.

The next three nights it was the same. Rod walked stone-faced and silent while Ross was just there for his brother. The next night before they could walk, Hugh came with Emily and Paula who urged Rod to come back to school. Rod refused.

"Will you pray the Our Father with me?" Hugh asked him.

Rod stared at his friend for a long time. Finally Hugh began the prayer and all joined in. When they had finished, Rod intoned the prayer again. They repeated and repeated for several minutes before Rod let them stop. He began to cry very softly. Paula and Emily each put an arm across his shoulders.

Noticing Needs

1) How is Ross helpful to his brother?

2) What sort of help does Rod need to get him back to school?

3) Do Sheila's other friends have deep needs of their own at this time? How might someone help them?

4) Are Hugh and Paula and Emily helpful to Rod? How?

5) What are some of the ways friends can help each other at times of great sorrow?

Putting Yourself in the Story

What would you do to be helpful to your friends if you were on the scene with Rod and Ross and the others?

PART TWO

Shaping Strategies

A helpful response plans a strategy that fits not only the *need* but also the *person* needing help.

The stories in this section invite the reader into dialogue with teens who are deciding how to help. These stories focus on the *techniques* of helping. In deciding how to help one must listen and watch sensitively. Clues to a helping response may be found in verbal or nonverbal cues. Young people need to learn to read both before they can decide how to help.

The stories in this section are designed to help teens consider the following points:

- how a decision to help might be made;

- how the decision to help was made in this story;

- how we decide what help is needed;

- how this process is modeled in the story;

- how the person needing help in the story is unique;

- how we could meet that uniqueness.

The Chip on Kirk's Shoulder

My name is Hank. Kirk and I have been going lots of places together for a long time now. Kirk has a habit of getting us into fights. The problem for me is that he is small and I am big. Kirk is five feet tall and very quick-tempered. Even in PE class he gets into it with somebody about once a week. He picks the fights and I have to get us out of the jams.

"I'll try to control my temper," he has said many times. But then he loses it again.

For instance, we went together to the county fair last month. We really had a lot of fun, but it was just the way it always was. I had to pull him out of two arguments with strangers. If somebody bumps him in a crowd, he can't just let it go. He has to say something tough. Then they have to say something back. If I hadn't been there he would have been eating his teeth. He knows very well that he is a little guy but he still wants to fight the world.

He got himself kicked out of biology lab for losing his temper. Another boy bumped his table as he walked along the aisle. "Hey, dummy," Kirk shouted, "you just ruined my work!"

Actually, it wasn't a big thing. Bumping the table did spill some stuff we were working with, but all we had to do was get some more and get it done. Kirk made such a scene of it that the teacher sent him to the office. He finally got permission to go in after school to make up the work.

Another silly thing he did happened in church. One Sunday we went early together; both our parents wanted to sleep in for a while. We were sitting in a full pew with some other people. Some lady tried to crowd into the seat by pushing Kirk. At first, he wouldn't move, but when she continued it was the same old thing.

"Okay, lady," he bellowed out loud, "you can have my place." He stomped out of the church grumbling to himself. She was embarrassed. I was embarrassed. People turned to stare at him. Kirk went home.

Another time he lost his temper in American history class.

No one, including Kirk, was sure what caused that incident. He ended up calling Mrs. Ross some names. That one got him a two-day suspension and he spent five days after school making up what he missed.

"I didn't mean to call Mrs. Ross all those names," he informed me. "She just made me so angry!"

Something happened yesterday which convinced me that Kirk can control his temper if he wants to. We were walking along a street. A little girl came roaring out of a driveway on her bike. She hit Kirk and knocked him down. I knew he was really hurting by the expression on his face and the way he was holding onto his leg.

She dropped the bike and ran to him repeating, "I'm sorry, I'm sorry!" Did Kirk snap? No. He looked at her as she came to him and then he reached up and gave her a hug.

"Don't cry," he said. "It's okay. I'm okay,"

I really like Kirk when his temper doesn't get in the way. He is a great storyteller and he must have read every joke book that has ever been printed. When he rattles off one story after another, I almost split laughing.

That's one of the reasons I like him so much.

Last weekend I stayed overnight at Kirk's house. It was one of the greatest nights we have ever had together. No fights! Kirk didn't flare up at his dad or his mom or me. We played pool, the four of us, on his dad's table. We watched a good movie his mom had rented on TV. His dad grilled hamburgers in the backyard and we ate sitting on the lawn—just like a picnic. It was hard to believe Kirk ever had trouble getting along with people.

Then two nights later we went jogging. As we trotted by one house, a big dog jumped up and barked at us. He really did scare us. His master called him and the dog sat down, but Kirk had to call the man names and threaten to "punch his lights out" if it happened again.

"Hey, Kirk, you must be crazy," I warned him. "If you even touched that fellow, his dog would eat you bite by bite."

When we got back to my house, I was still upset with him. I was about to lose my own temper. "Kirk, the next time you get us into some kind of fight, I'm going to join the other guys and pound on you," I threatened. "Maybe if you get a few good beatings, you'll find a way to handle your temper."

I paused for just a moment. "So now go home," I told him.

Shaping Strategies

1) Should Hank give up on Kirk and find other friends?

2) Is wanting to help Kirk a good thing? Should one friend always help another?

3) Is Hank exposing himself to too much fighting by continuing to see Kirk?

4) What are some dangers in fighting?

5) What is there about Kirk that makes him difficult to help?

6) How important is it to be able to exercise self-control? Can a person help someone else achieve self-control?

7) Should Hank seek assistance from some adult? If so, what adult?

Putting Yourself in the Story

If you were Hank, what would you do?

Too Little Time

When I came to the 10th grade at Edison High School, I felt lost. I had never moved before; it was awful not to know anyone at school. The first person who talked to me was Rhoda.

"What's your name?" she asked me.

"Heather," I replied.

As we went through the day, moving from class to class, I noticed that she was in all but one of my classes. She always said something to me, but she was not a very talkative person. In last period we sat across the aisle from each other. A few minutes after class started, I saw that Rhoda was fast asleep. I didn't know what to do. I just hoped no one else would notice. I felt bad—she had been so kind to me.

She didn't wake up even when the dismissal bell rang. I moved quickly across the aisle, caught her arm and woke her. She opened her eyes and gave me a funny smile. I guessed she was embarrassed.

"I fell asleep again, didn't I?" she asked.

"Again?" I repeated.

She gave me a broad grin. "Yes, again," she laughed. "You're new so you don't know that I do this sleepyhead act once in a while."

"Are you all right? You're not sick?" I inquired.

"No, just sleepy," she replied.

We left school together but went our own ways home. We lived in opposite directions from the school. The more I thought about it, the more I was convinced that Rhoda needed help. I determined to find out more.

The first thing I discovered was that Rhoda was the oldest of a very large family. They lived crowded into a small house. One day when Rhoda didn't have her homework, she explained that too many kids and too many distractions made it hard to find time for homework. At least, that was the case most of the time. "Most of the teachers have given up on me by this time," she added.

"Do you really believe that?" I asked.

"Oh, I know they have."

Before going to sleep that night, I thought about Rhoda and her difficulty with homework. I finally fell asleep when I decided that it would be almost impossible to help her. In the morning, I asked Mom if I could invite Rhoda to stay overnight.

"Sounds okay to me," Mom responded, "but make it Friday when there's no school the next day. And be sure Rhoda checks with her mom."

Rhoda did spend Friday night. It was the first real opportunity for the two of us to get acquainted. The time we spent together at school was only little snatches, and Rhoda always had to go right home after school. That Friday night we talked about many things.

Rhoda wore a great dress. I commented on it.

"Yeah, I like it, too," she said.

It was different. I had never seen one anything like it. "It's really unique," I said.

"One of a kind," she stated proudly. "My mom made it for me. She sews almost all our clothes."

"You usually wear slacks and jeans to school."

"Mom makes those for me, too. She gives me a hard time about them because I want them to be pretty much like what everyone else wears," Rhoda explained.

I learned that night why Rhoda always hurried home from school. She fixes dinner on weekdays so her mother can do other things for the family. After dinner, the younger kids help Rhoda with the dishes. After that, she has to do her homework in the middle of the whole noisy gang or wait until the younger ones go to bed before starting. I began to realize why she wasn't doing well in school.

"You're sure a lot busier than I am," I observed.

Later in the evening, I discovered that several other activities consume Rhoda's time. She baby-sits two nights each week for a neighbor. The money she earns buys material for her mother to make her clothes. In addition, she occasionally baby-sits at home to give her mom and dad a chance to get out.

That Friday night showed a lot about Rhoda. She had so little time for study or play, while I had almost nothing to do, no disruptions and all the opportunities of an only child. When she prepared to go home late Saturday morning, I learned something else about my friend.

"Thanks for asking me to stay over," Rhoda said to me. She hesitated a moment. "Maybe I shouldn't have come," she continued slowly. "I really had a good time, but there is no way I can ask you over. We just don't have any room."

I was dumbfounded. I just grabbed her and gave her a hug. "You're wonderful!" were the only words I could speak.

Shaping Strategies

1) Do Heather and Rhoda have enough in common to be close friends?

2) Is wanting to help Rhoda a good thing, or should Heather just let Rhoda live her own life? Why or why not?

3) Should one friend always help another?

4) Would Rhoda be difficult to help?

5) Should Heather tell their teachers about Rhoda's overload?

6) In attempting to help, are there some things Heather should not do?

7) Should Heather continue to invite Rhoda to visit even though Rhoda cannot return the invitations?

Putting Yourself in the Story

If you were Heather, what would you do?

The 'Build Bill' Team

I admit I have always been into some kind of mischief. The one thing I can't stand is boredom. If something isn't happening, I want to make it happen. I suppose that's why I set out to do something about Bill.

Bill was an average guy with average ability. There was nothing very striking about his appearance, but I was convinced that there could be. He was quiet—too quiet. He was so shy that he was almost not there. Once in a while he'd smile—a great smile that really lighted up his face. I just knew he could be such a neat guy if someone just got him going.

The first Saturday night in April Beth had invited Cindy, Mona, Susan and me to a slumber party at her house. "This may be our last slumber party in junior high," I suggested. "Maybe we should do something special."

"Okay, Becky, what have you got in mind?" Mona asked. I just shrugged.

"Come on, Becky. You always come up with the wild ideas," Cindy challenged.

I didn't have an idea then. We finally decided on an unusual scavenger hunt. We prepared the usual list of things to get, but chose not to compete with each other. Instead, the five of us went out as a team. It didn't take very long. We started right after supper and we had everything before nine o'clock.

Later, when we were settled on the rec room floor with, of course, no thought of sleep, I remembered Bill.

"Hey, listen," I announced. "This year has been a boring one at school. Do you agree?"

The ayes had it. "We're listening. What are you up to this time?" Susan baited me.

"I'll bet you have an idea," Mona added.

"I do have an idea. Let's form a 'Build Bill' team."

"A what?" they chorused.

First I described how Bill hardly made an impression on anyone. They agreed. Then I suggested that perhaps all he needed was a little help to get him out of his shell. They decided that I might be right. They wanted to know more.

"So what's this team business?" asked Beth.

"I'm not sure," I admitted. "We need to decide how we can help him."

After almost an hour, we tried to summarize our suggestions: "We wake him up, give him happy hellos. We all find ways to talk to him one on one. We ask him questions. We ask him for help. Maybe we even clap if he answers a question in class."

The team went into action Monday morning. We all spoke to Bill. We were delighted when he answered each of us with a separate hello that first morning. He reminded me of Bashful in *Snow White*. The next day, we each had a question ready to ask him. He answered all of us. We were sure our plan was working.

The third day, he seemed to resist our greetings. We had to work to get him to reply. When we tried questions, he simply told us he didn't know the answer. The questions weren't that difficult; we knew he was backing off. We decided that I would try to get into a conversation with him on the fourth day.

I tried. It went pretty well. He talked very quietly, even smiling now and then. I was encouraged. "Have you got your speech ready?" I asked.

He stared at me rather intensely. "You know, I hate giving a speech," he finally confessed.

"Oh, they aren't that bad," I commented.

"It's like having a bunch of girls trying to make you talk," he said. "I'm not crazy about that, either."

I wasn't certain how to take that remark. It took some fast thinking to come up with a reply. "You're not afraid to talk to girls, are you?" I queried.

He just looked down and avoided my eyes, then walked away.

After school I talked to Beth and Susan. I told them that my conversation with Bill had washed out. He had backed away. When I asked them what we should do, they both thought maybe we should drop the "Build Bill" team. I argued for continuing until they somewhat reluctantly agreed.

Bill still spoke to us if we greeted him, but otherwise he went back to being his shy self. Occasionally he would answer someone's question but usually he would shrug or say that he didn't know. I was frustrated and unhappy. It had seemed like such a good plan.

It was obvious that Bill was avoiding members of the team. He seemed quite satisfied to be not really there. I was upset that nothing had worked and a little uneasy for even having tried.

Shaping Strategies

1) Does Becky have the right to attempt to change Bill?

2) Are the team's efforts meant to make Bill a happier person?

3) Will changing Bill as the team wants to do make Bill better for himself?

4) Is the "Build Bill" team helping or harassing?

5) Should the team stop trying to help Bill when he backs away?

6) Should Becky try to help Bill overcome his discomfort with girls?

7) Should helping someone ever become a game?

Putting Yourself in the Story

What would you do if you were one of the team members?

Hidden Problem

My father was transferred here to become the general manager of his company's new plant. I had to make new friends in a new high school. That was a little scary, but Dad always taught my brothers and me that we should choose our friends rather than waiting for friends to choose us. "Pick the people you want to associate with," he'd say. "That way you end up with the friends you want and need."

So I told myself that moving was a real opportunity to try out his advice. I picked Mindy shortly after entering Jefferson High. She was a bright student with a contagious sense of humor. She didn't seem to have a problem in the world. It wasn't until we became close friends that she told me her father was an alcoholic and was causing his family an unbelievable amount of grief.

Mindy and I had a lot in common. I was a good student; she was straight-A. I was a better than average swimmer; she held state records in butterfly and breaststroke. I liked working backstage in plays; she was a talented actress. She liked to talk; so did I. We both liked every subject and every teacher on our 10th-grade schedules.

"Hey, Lisa, are your brothers both seniors?" Mindy asked when we were just getting to know each other.

"That's right," I replied. "Bob is actually a year older, but he was hurt in an auto accident. He missed almost a whole year of school, but he's better than new now."

"They're a couple of big, handsome guys," she whispered.

"Oh, you've noticed!" I joked.

That's the way it was almost from the first day we met. Mindy kept her big problem carefully hidden. I think I was the first person she ever told about her dad. She was always friendly and laughing with everyone—in class and out.

She didn't want anyone to know about her father. Naturally, I promised to tell no one. She told me she was glad she'd finally found someone she trusted enough to tell. At least she could talk to someone about her problem now. It was very hard to keep it completely to herself.

Mindy's grandfather, her mom's dad, had moved in just a short time earlier. He was a wealthy man whose life had spanned several careers. He was trying to find a way to rehabilitate her father. Most important to Mindy, Gramps was a lot like her. He had a delightful sense of humor which he used to keep her spirits up. He was also good for her mom.

When we got involved in the school play, Gramps began picking us up and taking us home. "Lisa, I understand you are an expert with paintbrushes and hammers," he teased me.

"Just an old stagehand," I sang back to him.

One night I got to the car a few minutes ahead of Mindy. The drama teacher wanted to check one of her lines with her. That gave Gramps a chance to talk to me.

"You're good for Mindy," he told me. "She needs a friend right now, as you know. I'm afraid she's getting a bit depressed. She tries to keep busy but sometimes her sadness creeps through."

"Is there something I should do to help her?" I asked him.

"Just be her friend," he replied.

It was frightening to hear him talk about depression. I was even more concerned when I heard a few days later that Mindy's father lost his job. The family apparently wouldn't be lost without his salary as long as Gramps was in the picture, but it still had a big impact on Mindy.

"I never really expected this to happen," she admitted to me. "Dad was in trouble with his drinking, but I thought he could still do his job. Mom told me that his boss called him in and told him he could no longer afford to have Dad around. Now he's drinking more than before."

"Is there something I can do to make it easier on you?" I asked.

"Right now, Lisa, nobody seems able to help," she answered. "Only Gramps."

"I really like him," I told her. "It's good for you to have him around."

"That's so right!" agreed Mindy. "I think I would have lost it if he hadn't come when he did."

We talked for a long time. I wasn't sure what I should do, but whenever Mindy felt like talking, I just listened. She began to sound tired, and that bothered me. The play did help. Mindy was totally into the production. She was good, too. It was fun just to watch how well she played her part. But when the play was over, I could smell trouble. Her major distraction was gone.

Mindy began to lose some of her sparkle and to have moody spells. It became harder and harder to help her shake off the blues. She seemed to lean on me more and more. Still somewhat new at the high school, I didn't know who else might be helpful. All this was something I never had to deal with and it was difficult to know what to do.

"What should I be doing?" I asked her grandfather again.

"Try to keep her smiling" was all he could tell me.

Shaping Strategies

1) Is it easier to help attractive friends than unattractive ones?

2) How can Lisa use the many interests she shares with Mindy to help her friend?

3) Exactly what kind of help does Mindy need?

4) Are another person's problems ever too personal for friends to try to help solve them?

5) Should Lisa talk to her father about the friend she has chosen? Why or why not?

6) Is there any danger that Lisa might try to help too much? Why or why not?

7) What other suggestions might Mindy's grandfather have offered Lisa?

Putting Yourself in the Story

If you were Lisa, what would you do to help Mindy?

A Family Affair

My name is Doris and I have a twin brother David. I had always known that David was very smart. Whenever I got stuck on some part of my homework, all I had to do was ask him for help. He would see right away what had to be done. He would help me understand and then I would be able to go on and finish it by myself.

His homework was different. He would do it on time, quickly and with no trouble. Then he would lose it or forget it and hand it in late. The teachers were forever comparing him to me and to our older brother and sister. We three had earned honor roll grades all through school. David seemed to gain attention, even though it was critical, by doing poorly in school.

David's only real interest in school was choral music. He has a fine voice, a big booming baritone voice. Other than this one subject, he gave the impression of total disinterest in school. He auditioned for the lead in the school musical and won it when he was only a sophomore. He was completely at home in his part. Teachers, students and parents all congratulated him on his performances on the two nights the show was presented. He took it all in stride. He knew he had done a good job.

"What does it feel like to be a star?" I teased him.

"I liked it," he replied seriously. "It was exciting. I was on a high every minute I was on the stage. Have you ever felt anything like that?"

His question stumped me for a minute. "I think so," I replied. "It happens to me when I get a report card with all A's."

"Doris! Not you, too."

Remorse hit me when I realized what he meant. "No! No!" I protested. "That's not what I wanted to say. I wasn't bugging you. I'm sorry. I really wasn't."

"Everybody bugs me," he laughed. "From you, I could take it."

"That's nice," I assured him. "Just remember I didn't mean to."

He could have been as good in all his studies as any one of us. His grades were always passing. For all his homework problems, he always got the top test score in the class. That combination of up and down performances usually netted him a C. When he got his report card, he'd just nod and smile. As long as he passed, it was all right with him.

Dad would ask, "Can't you do any better than this, David?" and David would answer, "Apparently not."

Dad would fume at that answer. "I was hoping for something better," he'd tell David.

"Yeah, I know," David would reply.

He knew exactly what Dad wanted—four for four on the honor roll. David never offered an alibi, never an excuse to explain why his grades were not higher and never a promise that they would improve. He seemed quite satisfied if he passed everything.

I seemed to sense in David a reaction, half hidden and half open. I was never certain, but I sometimes thought he got defensive about other people's expectations. But I had to dismiss that idea. Maybe because we're twins, we were often more aware of each other's feelings and thoughts than other people were. As a result, we were closer than most brothers and sisters. When I thought it through, I was positive that I would know if David was in any way defensive.

"I'm sorry Dad was upset with your report card," I told him after the last report period.

He gave me a little grin. "Thanks, twin. I understand Dad wanted all A's."

"I dare you to surprise him with two or three," I challenged, half joking.

David straightened up. "Aha! You are plotting in favor of our father," he said in that deep voice of his.

"I am not," I argued. "I am just trying to prove you can get as many A's as you want."

"You are a subtle rascal," he said, pretending to curl a mustache he didn't have.

There were other times I tried talking to him about getting better grades. He'd only tease me by saying that I sounded like one of his teachers.

"If I know the stuff, isn't that all that matters?" he would ask. "The grade doesn't make me any smarter."

"But do you know it?" I'd demand in frustration.

"Do I ever get a bad test score?" he would ask with a laugh.

One time I tried a different question. "Are you goofing up your grades just to torment all of us?"

He stared at me for a minute. "Hmmmm!" he said. That was all.

Next time report cards were coming, I knew I was getting one B. The logic of geometry was too much for my resisting mind. I had to keep telling myself that a B wasn't the end of the world. When it finally came, I really didn't mind. It made me smile to realize that I was thinking just like David. That made me wonder how he had done this time.

He brought his card to me. "This is for you," he said. "You can give it to Dad with your own. One thing though—this will be the only time. I promise you that."

I opened the report card. It was all A's.

Shaping Strategies

1) Should Doris have tried to interest David in improving his grades? Why or why not?

2) If David really is learning more than his grades indicate, should anyone be trying to change him? Why?

3) Since David's best talent and real interest is music, should he be concerned about anything else? Why?

4) Even though he seems to "know the stuff," should David be working for better grades? Why?

5) Does David appreciate his sister's efforts to help him? Should he? Explain.

6) Should Doris tell David to show his report card to their dad himself?

7) What should Doris say if she gives the report cards to their dad?

Putting Yourself in the Story

What would you do next if you were Doris?

No Fragile Flower

Tim and I were concerned about our friend Rose. Neither of us had known Rose before we met her in a summer tennis program last June. The next fall Rose and I entered 10th grade at Central High School where Tim was a junior.

Rose was a big, strong girl. She was by far the best athlete among the girls at the high school even though she was only a sophomore. Her continuous competition in athletics kept her hard and trim. At 6'1", with all her muscles, Rose had become the brunt of many unkind remarks. She began to avoid other students and was becoming more and more of a loner.

Rose was not particularly attractive. She was lanky and big-boned but, when she moved, Tim and I saw the grace of a swan and the spring of a tiger. Then she was beautiful. In addition, she was an above-average student. Each day Rose's attitude became more fiercely competitive. She seemed to focus on her ability to win. If people didn't want to be friendly and courteous, let it be. She knew she could overcome almost anyone in head-to-head competition. She was probably right, but Tim and I worried that she turned people off.

"Vicki, if they could just get to know her...," mused Tim.

"That's right. She is really a great person. But it seems to me that we have to help her help herself," I added.

Tim agreed.

For a charity drive the student council came up with the idea that Rose should run against the top boy on the cross-country team. She agreed—and she beat him. In some ways, this helped her. Upper-class females admired her victory and a number of them told her so. But such a reward also made tough competition even more important. Even in the classroom, Rose was zeroing in on other students. She was becoming ruthless in her determination to be first.

Tim and Rose were exactly the same height and, in a real sense, could see eye to eye. They had been mixed doubles partners in summer tennis.

"Hey, buddy," he teased her, "take it easy on all these little people. They need to see us tall ones as gentle giants."

"Tim, they're really getting to me," she admitted.

"I know. High school can be rough at times. Just don't let it get you down. It's not the end of the world if someone else wins once in a while."

He got her to smile, but the smile was soon gone. When one of the girls called her a horse, Rose reacted swiftly. With a backhand slap, she knocked the girl down.

Miss Wilton, a math teacher, intervened. "Carrie, go put cold water on your face," she told the girl. Miss Wilton is a very small woman. When she turned to Rose, she looked way up into Rose's angry eyes. The teacher panicked and hurried off down the hall.

I dragged Rose off to our next class, hoping it was all over. It wasn't. Carrie's parents made threats to sue Rose and the school. Miss Wilton asked that Rose be removed from her class. When Rose asked the counselor why he was moving her to another class, Mr. Evans laughed openly.

"Rose, I understand you're a tough competitor," he said. "Sit down for a minute and let's talk about it."

Rose told Tim and me later how Mr. Evans talked her through the difference between winning using brute force and using your head. She was grinning when she told us how he answered her question about changing classes.

"I'll tell you," Mr. Evans said, "but don't you tell it all over school. Miss Wilton thinks you came from outer space and might eat her alive in the middle of one of her parabolas. I just think I'd better get you out of there."

Whatever else Mr. Evans did, he had brought laughter out of Rose for the first time since summer. Tim and Rose and I went out and had a Pepsi together. We just needed to relax. As we talked, Rose told us she would be trying out for basketball and track. She was competing in cross country at that time.

"How about tennis in the spring?" asked Tim.

Rose frowned at him before she answered. "Probably not," she said simply.

I decided it would be best if I said nothing. I had said nothing to either Tim or Rose, but I had known for some time that two of the female tennis players were responsible for a good deal of the ridicule Rose had been suffering. I knew I would make the girls' tennis team. That meant that Rose would easily make it. She had apparently chosen to skip tennis. Tim didn't drop his question.

"Why not?" he inquired stubbornly.

Rose set her jaw. "I'm not going to tell you," she said, her eyebrows raised.

"So you don't like tennis anymore?"

"Didn't say that," Rose replied tersely.

Tim beamed a big grin at the two of us. "You won't play if you can't have me as a partner!"

Rose gave a little gasp. "Maybe I will play after all," she suggested.

"I hope so," Tim responded. "I want you ready for next summer."

Our party broke up. Later, Tim and I talked about Rose. "I'm not sure," he said, "just how much we're helping."

"I know," I added. "I'm not sure what to try next."

Shaping Strategies

1) Is it natural for Tim and Vicki to be concerned about Rose? Why?

2) Should Tim and/or Vicki have given more direct advice to Rose?

3) Rose may have a need for better interpersonal skills. How could Vicki or Tim help with this?

4) Should the counselor have taken Rose out of Miss Wilton's class? Was he helping?

5) What might Vicki and Tim do to help Rose help herself?

6) Does Rose recognize her positive qualities? Would it be helpful if she were more aware of these? How?

7) Would it be helpful if everyone refrained from teasing, name-calling, disparaging remarks and the like?

Putting Yourself in the Story

If you were Tim or Vicki, what would you do?

'Grow Up!'

Chuck was a flirt. All the girls loved him for it. He was interested in the debate team and girls, girls, girls! He was the only sophomore on the debate team. He did satisfactory work at school, but he was not working up to his ability. He could easily have been an honor student. Instead he coasted and played.

I'm Jennifer. I've known Chuck since sixth grade and I have always liked him a lot. Not a love affair or anything like that. We have been good friends. I knew he could do much better than he was doing. It made me unhappy to see him waste himself and his time. Even in the classroom he was always hard at work trying to entertain one or more of the girls. He was highly motivated when it came to debate and he was good. I wanted very much to help him get excited about the rest of his opportunities around school.

Chuck is a fun, happy-go-lucky guy. He makes people laugh, especially when they are down. Even some of the teachers have found Chuck very funny. At the same time, not even the teachers have found a way to turn Chuck's energies to something productive. To Chuck, life was a big laugh.

Two of his teachers made life very difficult for Chuck because of his lack of effort. He was in trouble with them because he refused to take anything seriously. They nagged him for his easygoing ways. Chuck shrugged it off and looked for something to make himself smile.

Early in the school year, the debate team coach had scheduled debates with five other high schools. Chuck and his partner had won all five of their appearances. Chuck used this success to heckle the teachers who were nagging him. "See, I work hard on my debates," he needled them.

His math teacher was not amused. "Passing this class is not open to debate!" he reminded Chuck.

Occasionally Chuck would take me out. He was always fun—except for one thing. I knew for sure that he would stop to talk to every other girl we met. Not just hello; he had to have a conversation with every one. Even though we're just friends, the way he carried on with other girls while he was with me seemed rude. If I'd had any serious thoughts about him, every date would have been a disaster for me. As it was, I wondered again and again about how to help a friend grow up.

It seemed as though it was time for him to begin growing up. Instead, he kept right on acting like a little boy, never serious about anything. He had so much ability but he just joked his way along. He always had plenty of money to spend because he worked 10 or 12 hours every weekend for his dad's trucking company. Apparently he worked hard and his dad paid him well because he would pass the rest of the week spending his money.

One day I went into the Pizza Palace after school. There he was sitting at a large table all by himself.

"Hi, Jennifer," he greeted me. "Come on and sit here with me." He caught my wrist and eased me down beside him. Just a minute later, Peg came along.

"Hi, Peg," he said. "Come on and sit here with me." He seated Peg next to me.

Before he got back to his own chair, there was Shirley. "Hi, Shirley. Come sit here with me."

In a matter of minutes, he had all the chairs at the table filled—himself and seven girls. His next move was to order pizza and pitchers of Coke for us all. That day he entertained us for over an hour with pizza and Coke and laughs.

As if things were not bad enough, Chuck had his 16th birthday and got his driver's license. He began taking his mom to work. That gave him her car every day to drive around an unbelievable assortment of girls. It seemed to me that he was headed for an even greater waste of his ability. All I could see was Chuck playing away every minute.

It became obvious to me that I could not help him. So I began to avoid him instead.

It was almost a relief to stop worrying about Chuck. I was busy with other things, including a part-time job at the fabric store. I liked sewing and the owner began teaching me a lot that I didn't know. Three weeks went by very rapidly. One evening I hurried home for supper and a couple hours of homework.

"Jennifer, Chuck was by this afternoon looking for you," Mom called to me.

"What did he want?"

"He didn't say," she answered.

As I finished supper, the doorbell rang. It was Chuck. I invited him into the living room. It was quiet there because Mom and my brothers were watching TV in the family room. Dad was at a meeting.

"Why have you been dodging me?" he asked.

"Have I been?" I countered.

"It seems that way," he accused.

I said nothing. After waiting briefly, he continued. "I've wanted to take you riding, but you haven't been around. In fact, you're the only one I've wanted to take riding."

Not knowing what to say, I decided to say nothing.

"I really mean that," he added.

It was surprising to hear Chuck talk about something in a serious tone. I realized that I was seeing a different Chuck.

"What do you say?" he asked.

Shaping Strategies

1) Does Chuck have a problem that requires help? If so, what?

2) Are Jennifer's concerns justified? Explain.

3) Would it be helpful for Jennifer to communicate her concerns and feelings directly to Chuck? Why?

4) What are some ways to help a friend "grow up"?

5) Chuck has his own way of pursuing popularity. How is it good? How is it bad?

6) Do you think peer pressure is helping or hurting Chuck? Explain.

7) Does it really matter if a friend of yours is performing far below his or her ability? Why?

Putting Yourself in the Story

If you were Jennifer, how could you help Chuck now?

'I Never Kiss Boys!'

Clare was a loner. She really seemed to have no friends. I'm just the opposite. Everyone is my friend; old Zach, they call me! I knew better than half the people in my high school and all the people in my class. Everyone but Clare, that is. Nobody knew Clare. She seemed shy or something. She'd come to school every day, but you couldn't talk to her. I would speak to her and get nothing back but a little mousy hello. For me that's really a failure.

Clare was prettier than most girls. She had a nice face and a nice figure and nice hair. But she wouldn't talk—not to anybody. The only activities she ever attended were athletic events. Then she sat alone or sometimes with one other girl. I was sure that girl didn't attend our school. She either went to another high school or was out of school. She looked a little older.

It was hard to believe any student at Roosevelt could be so isolated. While we had a big enrollment, the spirit was great. We had more smiles and laughs per square foot than you could count. Most of the teachers really knew their way around and you could learn about as much as you were willing to learn. In the middle of all this, we had Clare, the lost one.

Last year I saw her at most of the football and basketball games. The night of the last football game Clare was there alone. She sat there, not talking to anyone, just watching the game. I watched her more than I watched the game. She distracted me that much. I kept thinking that there must be something I could do to help Clare.

It was a very dark night with lots of heavy clouds and lots of wind. When the teams returned to the field for the second half, the winds came in stronger gusts and all the lights went out. I looked behind the stands and saw that the street lights were out down the street. Everyone sat there in the dark, making smart remarks or tickling some girl so she'd scream. Finally someone began walking in front of the stands with one of those battery-operated horns telling everyone to go home. The second half would be played another day.

As I approached the gate I could barely make out Clare's face beside me. I looked several times to be certain. I spoke to her.

"Come on, Clare, I'll walk you home. It's awful dark."

She stopped, standing stiffly without replying. I have always been too outgoing or aggressive or something to let things stop me. I grasped her arm and began guiding her through the gate. Once we were outside, she walked beside me in the dark. A minute or so later I took her hand and tucked it into my arm. "When a girl walks with me, she holds my arm," I said, laughing.

If I asked a question as we walked, she answered but she didn't say anything more than she had to. She told me where she lived and after a lot of blocks we arrived there.

"There!" I said. "I got you home safely. Do I get a goodnight kiss?" I felt her stiffen.

"I never kiss boys!" she snapped.

Her tone of voice was unnecessarily sharp. It caught me by surprise and I searched for an answer. I flipped out a remark. "No? Only girls?"

She sighed, then asked, "How did you know?"

"How did I know...?" I couldn't think what to say for what seemed a very long time. She went back into that silence of hers. Finally, when I couldn't stand not talking, I tried again.

"Wow!" I said. "You mean...? The way you said it.... I was just joking. I really didn't know anything."

"You do now," she declared firmly. "I think I'm becoming a lesbian—or maybe I already am one."

We both stood silent after that. Clare finally broke the silence. "I think I'm glad somebody knows."

"I don't need to tell anyone."

She patted my arm. "I'd appreciate it if you didn't," she said.

I wanted to help her. I had a strong impulse which I justified with the thought that maybe it wouldn't hurt anything. I reached out, held her and kissed her.

"Goodnight," I said softly. She retreated into the house and I walked home in the dark.

Next Monday I went to see Dr. Korski, the school counselor. I told her everything as it had happened except Clare's name. "I'm worried," I explained. "I don't want to be messing around and hurting this girl. What if she is a lesbian?"

"You really don't know that," Dr. Korski reminded me.

"Might I hurt her?" I asked.

"Zach, we never hurt anyone by being nice to them." That made me see something very important.

"Will you eat with me?" I asked Clare in the school cafeteria on Tuesday.

"I guess so," she replied tentatively.

We got our trays and sat down at an empty table. I figured no one would join us because of Clare's aloofness. I was glad when no one did because I wanted to talk to her.

"You've never had anything to do with boys?" I asked.

"Never," she replied simply.

"Okay, I have a proposition. Have three dates with me. Then if you want, I'll get you dates with a couple other guys. Then if you decide you only want to kiss girls, we'll let it be."

She stared at me across the table.

"Will you do it?" I grinned at her.

"I'll try one date first," she said.

"Okay. I can probably use Dad's car Friday night. We can go to an early movie."

"I'll tell you tomorrow," Clare promised.

Shaping Strategies

1) Is Zach's plan for helping Clare a good one or is he intruding into Clare's privacy?

2) What does Zach see as Clare's needs before walking her home from the game? After asking for a kiss?

3) What prompts Zach's desire to help Clare? Would you feel the same way?

4) Most of Clare's classmates seem willing to let Clare remain in isolation. Is this attitude good or bad? Why?

5) Is Zach's willingness to keep secret Clare's suspicions about herself helpful? Why or why not?

6) Was Zach right to consult Dr. Korski? How does this fit into a pattern of helpfulness?

Putting Yourself in the Story

What would you do now if you were Zach?

A Worrisome Friend

My name is Eddie. My best friend is Paul. We went all through elementary school together. When we finished the sixth grade summer before last, we both won a three-week trip to science camp. The last three summers we have made camping and fishing trips with our dads. The four of us have really had fun.

Then when we were halfway through eighth grade, trouble began. Paul still saw me, but he also had a new group of friends. What bothered me was that he told me they smoked pot. He wanted me to try it too.

I didn't like what was happening to Paul. In the cafeteria he sometimes didn't eat his lunch. Sometimes he really looked sick. When I asked him if he was all right, he'd say something like, "I partied too much last night."

We both played on a soccer team. Paul was a great player. Trouble was he started missing practices and even missed one game. The coach was ready to drop him. Paul was really hurting our team.

All that really bothered me. I told Paul he was nuts and he had better quit messing with drugs. He grumbled and told me to grow up. He went out at night a lot. Paul told me, "I tell my parents I'm going to your house."

He didn't study any more. He was still a good student but not as good as he had been. Lots of times he was too tired to pay attention. Or he goofed around so much that he had no time for his homework. Maybe he just didn't care.

In our life science class one week, our teacher played the Bill Cosby recording talking to kids about drugs. Everybody liked it— everybody except Paul, I guess.

"Old Cosby was a real comic, wasn't he?" Paul asked me.

It made me angry. "Listen, Paul, he wasn't being funny," I snapped at him. "He was very serious about a very serious problem."

Paul stared at me blankly, the way he does a lot these days. "Hey, Eddie," he said. "Why don't you try just one joint with me? Then you won't be telling me to quit. I know you'll like it."

"No way," I answered him. First of all, I guess I was afraid to try it. As I thought about it, I wondered if there was a danger that Paul might convince me. I didn't think so then, but when he kept asking it really began to worry me.

Going to his house wasn't the same anymore. Paul wasn't the same. He was jumpy and cross. He didn't even like TV most of the time. I had the feeling he saw me as an obstacle to getting out somewhere.

I really didn't know what to do. It scared me to be around him. But if I just quit seeing him, that would be abandoning him. On the other hand, just hanging around was no answer because I didn't know what to do. While I was worrying about how to help Paul, a guy stopped me a block away from our school.

"Hey, kid, your buddy Paul said you might want some of these," he said.

When I looked down at his open hand, I saw that he was holding two joints in his palm. I wanted to flatten him, but he was a lot bigger than I am. So I decided to do something different.

"Not interested," I declared. "I already know where to get all I need."

That didn't stop him. "I can beat the price," he argued.

"I'm sure you can't," I said. Without giving him a chance to say anything more, I walked quickly away. As soon as I knew I was clear of him, I went looking for Paul, who laughed at my being mad.

"I thought you might want your own. Besides, if I get him a new customer, I get a bonus!" Paul boasted.

"You don't need any bonus, Paul. You've smoked too much already," I grumbled back at him.

Even as the words came out of my mouth, I knew that it was the wrong approach. I was right. Paul got mad.

"Eddie, don't pull your saint act on me. It's only pot; I don't use the hard stuff. If I want to quit, I'll quit. Right now I don't want to, so I don't need you and your little sermons. You get me?" he bellowed.

"Hold it, Paul," I interrupted him. "We've been friends for a long time. You are still my friend, but you're making a mess of yourself. You're hurting the soccer team and you're slipping in school. If I didn't care, I'd forget you in a minute. I do care and I want to help you. You get me?"

Paul stared at me as though his sudden outburst had almost exhausted him. We stood face-to-face for a minute or so. Then he turned slowly and walked away. When he had taken a dozen steps, he turned his head over his shoulder.

"See you later, Eddie," he called in a sad voice.

"See you," I said around the lump in my throat.

Paul and I spoke when we met at school for the next two weeks, but we didn't ever get together. I was convinced that any chance to help him had vanished. I felt bad, but what could I do?

I was surprised when he came to talk to me one day. "Eddie, will you give me a hand?" he asked.

"Sure!" I answered.

"Could you lend me five bucks?" he mumbled.

"For more pot?" I asked him.

"Well, yeah," he admitted.

"Sorry, Paul, I'm broke." I had just earned $10 for cleaning a neighbor's yard. It made me feel even worse when I lied to Paul.

Shaping Strategies

1) Should Eddie give up on Paul?

2) Is wanting to help Paul a good thing? Should one friend always help another?

3) Is Eddie exposing himself to possible drug use by continuing to see Paul?

4) Can you help a friend who doesn't want your help?

5) Should Eddie tell the soccer coach, the science teacher or Paul's parents what is happening and ask them to help?

6) What are the dangers in experimenting with drugs (even "only" pot)?

7) What enables people to say no?

Putting Yourself in the Story

If you were Eddie, what would you do next?

No Joke

My name is Sarah and I'm in ninth grade at Columbus Junior High with my friend Megan. We spent hours just talking with each other at school, at home or wherever we might be. It was always fun to be with Megan, a real peppy person. By ninth grade she was a knockout with the greatest personality—more exciting every day. The boys hung around her in throngs.

One day we were standing by the locker we shared. It was right after school and Aaron, a 10th-grade jock, was behind us, putting books into his locker. Megan winked at me.

"Hey, I was watching Aaron in math today," she said loudly enough for him to hear. "All muscles and what a hunk. I'd go to third base with him anytime!"

Aaron slammed the locker door. He was blushing when Megan turned around and began to giggle.

"Oops!" she said, as if it had been an accident.

Aaron left quickly, probably for football practice. I was still trying to believe my ears. "Megan, why did you say that?" I asked. "You're not that kind of girl."

"Don't be too sure," she laughed.

I suddenly knew she meant it. I was her friend. I felt like I had to change her mind.

The next afternoon Megan didn't come to the locker at the end of the day. I guessed she had a conference with one of her teachers. I had to go to the dentist, and I needed to get home as quickly as possible. I left without talking to her.

When I met her in the morning, I asked where she had been. She just smiled and said that she would tell me about it later. Since we had different first-period classes, we had to go in opposite directions.

"Hey, I'll buy you a Coke after school," she called back to me.

Our favorite place to go was McDonald's. Megan picked out a booth and tossed her pack onto the seat.

"You want anything to eat?" she inquired.

"Just a large Coke," I replied.

She went to the counter and picked up our drinks and got some fries which I helped eat. A bit later, I issued a reminder. "All right, mystery lady, where were you yesterday?" I asked.

At first she gave me a smug little grin. She followed that with a simple statement: "With Aaron."

After waiting for her to say more, I pushed her with another question. "Is that all you're going to tell me?"

Megan leaned back, sipping slowly on her straw. "Nope, I'm going to tell you everything," she promised. She nibbled thoughtfully at the last french fry, took another sip of her Coke and leaned toward me.

"Aaron got excused from football practice. I don't know what reason he gave. The coach excused him because they don't have a game this week. Then we went to his house. His parents never get home before six so we had the house all to ourselves. I was scared at first but he was nice...really kinda shy." She gulped a deep breath. "So, Sarah, I've been to third base!"

My first reaction was to be angry with her. I felt like she had let me down, but I didn't say that. I only asked what had made her do it.

"He asked if I had guts enough to do what I said at the lockers. I just nodded yes. He hesitated and I almost backed out. Then he said that the last one ready was a wimp. It was a tie. We got all our clothes off at the same time."

Megan stopped to take a couple more sips of her Coke. "We got into bed," she continued. "We hugged and wrestled and touched each other. He kissed me. Then he turned on the stereo and we danced. We kissed some more. Then he said he was getting too excited and we'd better stop so we got dressed. He walked me home."

"I thought you were joking when you said you'd go to third base with him," I observed.

"No joke. Fooling around was fun. No risk. Just fun. I hope we do it again!"

"Megan! You don't!"

I knew exactly how I felt, but I just couldn't find the words to say it to Megan. We walked home together without saying much.

The next week Mandy, who spends a lot of time with both Megan and me, came up to me. "Sarah, you look down," she said.

"Did Megan tell you what she did?"

"Yeah, she told me," Mandy answered, "but Aaron is cute. I'd like to see him without his clothes."

"You, too?" I gasped.

"No, I'd chicken out," Mandy admitted. "I wouldn't do it, but I'd still like to see him."

"You wouldn't do it because you're scared?"

"Yeah. How about you, Sarah?"

"I think it's wrong," I replied.

"Like it's a sin?"

"I'd just feel dirty if I did it. And I think Megan has some real doubts."

"She told me they were going to get together again," Mandy said.

"I know that's what she says. I'm not sure either of them wants to."

"Then why plan it?" asked Mandy.

"Everybody knows about it. Now they think they have to."

Mandy frowned. "It's too bad somebody can't talk them out of it," she said.

"Yeah," I agreed. "But after they've gone this far, the only thing left is to go all the way!"

Shaping Strategies

1) Exactly what sort of help does Megan need? What does Aaron need?

2) Are there ways that Aaron and Megan could help each other?

3) Should Sarah have done something to try to help Megan when Megan said, "Don't be too sure." What might she have done at that time?

4) Now that "they think they have to," will it be more difficult for Sarah to help Megan?

Putting Yourself in the Story

If you were Sarah or Mandy, how would you help Megan?

PART THREE

Evaluating Efforts

A good helping effort neither takes full responsibility for meeting a need nor makes the other bear total responsibility for fulfilling a need.

The stories in this section invite the reader into dialogue with teens who are trying to help others. These stories provide exercises in evaluating helping efforts. Young people need to learn how to decide for themselves whether a helping effort is capable of positive impact.

The stories in this section are designed to help teens consider the following points:

- how to evaluate a helping effort;

- how to judge an effort that seems only partly helpful;

- how to judge an effort that does not seem to have helped at all;

- deciding how important the attitude of a would-be helper is;

- evaluating the efforts in these stories.

A Fall From the Top

I wasn't ready to run for class president. In fact, I hadn't considered it at all. One of the teachers pushed me, saying I needed leadership experience. Some of the freshmen agreed with her, so I agreed to be a candidate.

It was a new experience. The only elections I had ever seen were those where the teacher tallies the ballots on the chalkboard in front of the class. This election involved a complete campaign with speeches to a special freshman assembly. There were handouts and posters; bulletin boards were loaded with information about the people on the ballot. It was exciting.

Winning capped the experience. If this was leadership experience, I liked it! Beating the other two candidates for president gave me a sense of pride that I had never known at any other time.

The next morning a voice behind me said, "Congratulations, President Mike!" I turned to see Karen, who had been a classmate all through grade school.

"Thank you," I said.

"I always knew you'd be a big shot someday," she teased.

"That reminds me—I have to appoint a committee for the Oktoberfest Dance. Would you like to be the first committee member?"

"Oh, what an honor! What do I do?" she mocked my appointment.

"I don't know. I still have to find out."

Our class sponsor Mr. Kolter didn't let me wait long to find out. We quickly did an informal survey about what band students liked best. We decided the decorations for the hall. I appointed a subcommittee to be responsible for the decorating. Four of us had an appointment with the band we hoped to hire. Things were going very well. I was eating up this leadership stuff.

"Next committee meeting will be after school on Friday," I told them before adjourning the meeting.

Then I began to discover the dark side of leadership. Some people weren't happy with the band we hired and accused me of railroading. Once or twice I heard a voice in the hall between classes: "Make way for Mr. Important!" Some people even turned the other way when I came near. I tried to ignore it. After all, I'd done my best to please the class, and no one can please everybody.

The night of the dance came. Mr. Kolter told me how pleased he was with everything. The principal went out of his way to say he was proud of the fine job I had done. Some juniors and seniors came around to give me a pat on the back. I began to realize how important my leadership was to this event. Alicia came to me near the main exit doors.

"Nobody picked up the punch bowl," she advised me.

"Where is it?" I asked.

"Just down the street. Mrs. Kelly is lending it to us."

"I'll get it right away," I promised.

When I returned, the hall was beginning to fill. The band was there and had started to tune up. The punch bowl had to go to the corner diagonally opposite the entrance. I could have walked around, but I was feeling very important. I wanted to be seen. The best way to do that was to walk across the floor. When I reached the exact center of the floor, I stepped on something. My feet went up and I went down, flat on my back. My first thought was the punch bowl.

"I've got to catch that bowl," I thought to myself. "It must have cost a lot."

I caught it. The guy with the trumpet blew a fanfare. The crowd laughed and many of them applauded. "I could kill that guy with the trumpet," I thought. "I wish I could crawl off this floor." Then I reached a decision: "I'll give somebody this bowl and then I'm going home."

As I walked toward the table, I saw Karen standing there. She looked angry. I wondered if she was mad at me. She took the bowl just as the band began its first number and handed it to Alicia.

"You promised me a dance," she said. "I want it now."

"Going out there again is the last thing I want to do," I protested. "I'd probably fall down again!"

"Don't take it so seriously," she cautioned. "Come on. You owe me this one."

We danced once around the floor without saying a word. Then she looked up at me. "Smile for me," she said. "Not everybody applauded. Anyway one embarrassing moment isn't the end of the world."

Shaping Strategies

1) Was the approach Karen used after Mike's fall a good effort to help? Why?

2) What are some other examples of helping in this story?

3) Did the teacher who encouraged Mike to run for president help him? Explain.

4) No one went to Mike when he fell. Was this a missed opportunity to help? Why or why not?

5) Would Mike have helped himself if he had refused to dance with Karen and gone home? Why or why not?

Putting Yourself in the Story

If you were Mike, what would you do next?

'Get With It!'

I watched Patsy as she walked toward me. I wished I could show that much spirit when I walk. "Hi, Patsy!" I called when she got close.

"Hi, Brenda," Patsy grinned. I looked at that grin. She never seemed to have a care. She just smiled, no matter what the circumstances. She always listened, too. That made it easy to tell her all my troubles. "How come you look so down, Brenda?"

"My little brother got picked up for shoplifting. Everyone seems to know. It's embarrassing."

She just looked at me for a minute, like she was thinking. Her smile faded a little, but it never disappeared completely. "It must be embarrassing," she said. "Listen, Brenda, maybe we can help him so he won't do it anymore."

It seemed so hard to think about helping him; I wanted to smack him. I was hurt and angry. Besides, I had so many other problems that he was just going to have to get out of trouble on his own.

"On top of that, my older brother had another accident with my dad's car. Dad is furious. There's nothing but trouble at home!"

Patsy patted my shoulder. "Listen, look at it this way," she said. "Most dads would be angry with a brother who wrecked the car." Then like she always does, she smiled. I sure wanted to smile with her.

"Brenda, you'd feel better if we tried to help your little brother. We can make him realize that shoplifting is wrong," Patsy said.

I felt pushed, and that was the last thing I needed. The worst part of it was that I knew she was right. Maybe we could help, but there were other things that bothered me.

"Patsy, lay off. I'm not in the mood! I wish my mom and dad wouldn't fight every night. All these things make home a terrible place to be."

That didn't bother Patsy too much either. She looked straight at me, the way she looks at a tough math problem. It made me squirm a little. "I know it must be awful," she said slowly. "Could you sleep over with me tonight? I'm sure my mom would say yes."

That wouldn't solve the problems, but it sounded good at the time. We did our homework together. After that we relaxed on her bed and listened to her radio—probably later than we should have. I smiled some for the first time in several days.

"Patsy, you're my best friend," I told her.

"Thanks," she grinned. "I like you, too."

The next week or so things seemed to get worse for me in a lot of ways. My big test in history came back with a D on it. That was bad enough, but the teacher added a sarcastic remark. In math, I'm almost lost. Sometimes it's impossible to concentrate on the stuff. In English, I always misspell a lot of words; my papers come back so red they look like they are bleeding. To top things off, I finally got angry enough that I punched another girl right in the nose in gym. I thought the teacher was going to hit me.

"None of my teachers like me," I argued with Patsy. "I'm dumb and they only like smart kids."

Patsy's face lost its usual smile. She almost looked fierce as I faced her. She took a deep breath. "Brenda, we have to get one thing straightened out first," she whispered, the words coming at me one at a time. "You are not dumb. You're down, unhappy in class. You perk up and participate and you'll see a big difference!"

Patsy didn't smile much the next few days. It began to bother me, so I finally spoke to her about it. "You mad at me?" I asked.

"No, I'm just waiting for you to get with it," she replied.

That was the only time I can remember getting angry with her. "Get with it?" I snapped. "How do you know what problems keep me from getting with it?"

"You've always told me when you had a problem," she responded. "You haven't told me so you don't have a problem."

I felt just like I did before I punched the girl in gym. "That's all you know," I growled. "Bill asked me to the homecoming dance and I wanted to go with him so bad. My mom says if I need a dress I can't go. She can't afford it." We faced each other. "So that's why I don't feel like getting with it. Okay?" I challenged her.

She was giving me that math-problem look again. It felt like she might be measuring me. Then I understood.

"You are the very same size as my big sister," she said. "She left some nice dresses when she went to college. Mom would give you one of those."

"Thanks," I told her, "but I don't think so."

"Come look at them. Then say yes or no."

I looked at them. I tried on a very pretty one and I wore it to the homecoming dance. It was the biggest night of my life and it carried me through the next four weeks. Then Bill began to date somebody else, things got worse at home again and I made a big decision. It was hard, but I had to tell Patsy.

"You're my best friend," I began. "You're the only one I'm going to tell about this. Patsy, I can't find anything to like here at school or at home. I hate this town. That's all there is. I'm going to run away."

I thought she would get excited or angry. She didn't. She just accepted what I had told her quietly, not saying anything for at least a couple of minutes. "Hey, you're too smart for that," she finally began. "You've heard some of the terrible things that happen to runaways. It may be bad here, but that's much worse."

We talked for a long time that day, and the next, and the next. I'm still having a tough time, but I'm still here. It's been over a month since I decided to run away, but I haven't packed yet.

Shaping Strategies

1) Was Patsy's approach a good effort to help Brenda? Explain.

2) What problems do you think bothered Brenda most? What could a teen do about these problems?

3) Do we always have a responsibility to help someone else? Could we just let someone run away? Explain.

4) What actions might teens take to discourage someone from running away?

5) Many runaways are attempting to escape repeated failure and frustration. What are some ways helpers might provide experiences of success?

Putting Yourself in the Story

If you were Patsy, what would you do next?

The Torch

Stan and I had been friends for over two years, starting back in the ninth grade. One night we stood together watching the firefighters battle a fire. There was a big vacant lot between us and the old frame house that was completely in flames. The police had stretched a rope across the streets and along the length of the lot. Stan and I stood holding the rope in our hands as we watched.

"Boy, I hope no one was in there," I said.

"There wasn't, Toby," Stan declared firmly. "It was just an old vacant house. It has been empty for two years."

It was after midnight when we walked away. What had been a house was by then a pile of black sticks, smoldering and hissing as the hoses continued to spray water over the ruins. Stan's house was just three blocks away. We sat on his front steps for a few minutes, still talking about the fire. After that, I went on home.

The next afternoon I went over to see Stan. We sat on the old bench in his backyard, enjoying the shade that covered the spot and cooled the effect of the hot summer sun. Stan seemed to want to talk more about the fire. He kept coming back to it each time our conversation strayed away.

"That fire last night," he finally said. "I have to tell you something about it."

"You back on that?" I laughed.

Stan was serious. "Yeah, Toby, back on that," he repeated. "I have to tell you. I fired that house."

I thought maybe I hadn't heard right. "You've gotta be kidding!" I exclaimed.

"Nope. I fired it."

"Why?" I inquired in astonishment.

"I don't know. Maybe I wanted a thrill. I wasn't thinking. I don't know," Stan mumbled.

"Man, what a dumb thing to do!" I commented.

Stan sat up quickly. "You won't turn me in," he pleaded.

"Oh, I won't. Not right away anyway. I'm not sure what to do."

"Just don't turn me in," he repeated.

"Why did you tell me?" I questioned in frustration. "I didn't have to know about this."

"I had to tell somebody. You're the only one I trust," Stan responded.

"That's great!" I said, then paused. "First thing. If there's another fire, I will turn you in. You understand?"

That night, I didn't sleep very much. I wanted to help Stan, but I didn't know what I could do. The next day, he came to my house. We sat in my room. Stan closed the door.

"I don't think I'll ever do it again," he told me. "I just wanted to fire one old vacant building."

"How can you be sure? How can I be sure?" I asked.

"I'm telling you. I told you I did it. If I was going to do it again, I wouldn't have told you."

When Stan left and I was alone again, I went back to wondering what I should do. Then I remembered the house down in the next block. There was an office in the home with a side door of its own. On the wall beside that entrance was a small sign. It said: George Blain, Ph.D., Clinical Psychologist. I had heard once that psychologists fixed people who were mixed up. Surely Stan was mixed up! After a while, I decided to explore the possibilities.

By then it was late afternoon. When I tried the office door, it was locked. I knocked. A tall man came and opened the door. He looked at me with very serious eyes. "Good afternoon, young man," he greeted me.

"Hi. I'd like to talk to you for five minutes if you can spare it," I told him.

He stepped aside and pointed to the chair next to his desk. When we were both seated, I told him about the fire and about Stan, being very careful not to say anything that would give him any idea who Stan was. I finished and waited.

"And you want me to help your friend?" he queried.

"Yes," I replied. Then I thought I had better make something clear to him. "Yes, that's what I'd like, Mr. Blain, but he hasn't got any money and neither do I."

The psychologist smiled. "I understand," he said. "Get your friend to go to police headquarters. Do you know where that is?"

"I know," I answered.

"Go to Lieutenant Glover. He's in charge of juvenile affairs.

After your friend turns himself in, I'll call Glover. We work together a lot. He'll send your friend to me. I'll try to help him."

"How can I be sure of that?" I asked.

He shrugged his shoulders slightly. "You can't," he replied. "You either trust me or you don't."

"I don't think he'll go. I'm not sure I want him to," I spoke slowly, almost to myself.

He reached across the corner of the desk and put his hand on my arm. "That's it," he said. "Either he goes or you can't help him and I can't help him."

Shaping Strategies

1) Has Toby been making a good effort to help Stan? Explain.

2) Can Toby help Stan without help from someone else? Why or why not?

3) Who besides the psychologist could Toby have approached for help?

4) Toby says to Stan: "Why did you tell me? I didn't have to know." What do you think he meant?

5) Are there legal implications for Toby if he continues to cover for Stan?

Putting Yourself in the Story

If you were Toby, what would you do next?

Old Friends

My name is Sally. Twelve of us had been classmates all the way from kindergarten. Now we were in the 10th grade together. It was great to have that many people around that you knew well enough to talk with about anything. We had a very unusual friendship.

I was dating Josh, a big, good-looking senior. I liked him from the beginning. Only one thing bothered me. He kept wanting me to do things that I should not and would not do—drink, try drugs. I said no, but he kept on dating me and I kept going out with him.

I talked to my friends about him. Once he had some pot and wanted me to smoke with him. I said no. He didn't smoke his either, but he took me home early.

"Are you sure he really had marijuana?" Doris asked.

"Not absolutely, but he has had them before. Joints, he called them."

"I don't think you should go out with that guy anymore, Sally," Rita advised.

"Yes, Mamma," I teased her.

"Listen, we're old friends and I don't like this," she added.

"I understand and I'll behave," I promised.

After that, Josh and I had some dates that were really fun. He was funny and a real joy to be with. I liked him more each time we went out. Then something ugly happened.

Josh took me out for ice cream. "Hey, Sally, I'm house-sitting on Friday, Saturday and Sunday," he told me. "My aunt is going to be out of town for the weekend. She doesn't want the house empty so she's paying me to stay in it."

I laughed. I hadn't heard of house-sitting before then.

"It gives us a real opportunity," he said.

"What do you mean?" I asked him.

"You know what I mean. Friday night we can have the house to ourselves. It's a perfect chance to sleep together."

At first, I was too surprised and angry to speak. Then I surprised myself at how coldly I handled the situation. "Please take me home," I said.

"Hey, wait a minute. I thought you'd like the idea," he stammered.

"Then you thought wrong. Please take me home," I demanded. When I talked to Amy and Rita the next day, I wasn't going to tell them about it. After a while, I changed my mind.

They were both angry with Josh. Each of them told me not to see him anymore. The advice was really unnecessary since he practically disappeared for over two weeks. He used to find ways to meet me around school but that stopped entirely. The one time I saw him he turned and walked away without speaking.

"So much for that," I said to myself.

About two weeks after that one of the senior girls called me aside. She said she wanted to tell me something. "Josh is bragging to some of the seniors about how he's gotten everything he wanted from you. He says he doesn't need to date you any longer." She said she was sorry and added that she thought he was a rat. I just thanked her.

A short time later I found out what had happened. Amy made a slip and I made her tell me the whole thing. My friends of the last 10 years had decided that Josh was a bad influence on me. They didn't like the things he wanted me to do. In a way, they were right. But I had always said no to his push for drugs and booze and sex.

"You know how big and strong Rob and Jody are," Amy told me. "Well, they went to see Josh. They told him to stop seeing you. If he didn't, they would flatten his handsome face."

"But I didn't ask for this," I protested.

"We know," Amy insisted, "but we couldn't just stand by and let a...a...a jerk like Josh hurt you."

"But he didn't hurt me," I argued.

"Probably not, but he would have if you had kept on seeing him. We all wanted to help you."

Amy was nearly in tears so I thanked her and left. I was very angry at first. I walked blocks and blocks out of my way home to give me more time alone to think. The more I thought about the situation, the harder it was to decide. I knew that they all loved me. I knew that they all wanted to help me.

"But they were butting into my private life." I said it out loud even though the street was deserted. It had more emphasis that way. My anger and tension began to soften when I remembered how much I prized the friendship the 12 of us shared. One question stuck with me the rest of the way home: When do you accept help from friends and when do you tell them to get lost?

Shaping Strategies

1) Was the approach of Sally's friends a good effort to help? Why or why not?

2) Are long-time friends apt to be different in the way they help? Why?

3) Was the senior girl who came to Sally helpful? Explain.

4) How would you answer Sally's question: "When do you accept help from friends and when do you tell them to get lost?" Explain your answer.

5) How did Sally help herself?

Putting Yourself in the Story

If you were Sally, what would you do next?

The Color Barrier

I'm Lyle, and I guess I'm a racist. I never meant to be. I always thought I could get along with anyone. At least, that's what I thought when I lived in all-white neighborhoods and attended all-white schools. Then we moved, and suddenly I was in a school where almost half the students were black. I wasn't ready for the way I felt around black people.

In the first week of school, for instance, I was sitting on the low wall that runs along the sidewalk to the front entrance to the school, talking with two new friends. Four black students spoke to one of my friends and, before I knew what was happening, sat down with us. I was so uncomfortable I finally had to leave. I began then to wonder whether I would be able to have any friends in my new school.

A couple weeks later I had a problem in math class. Math had always been my favorite subject. We had a good teacher and I got off to a fast start. In just two weeks, I was identified as one of the top students in the class. There were quite a few blacks in algebra, whom I quietly ignored. Janella, a girl who sat across the aisle from me, refused to stay invisible.

"Lyle, you're really good in math," she said. "I wonder if you would give me some help sometime. I'm so confused."

I stared at her for a moment, not knowing what to say. Then I answered. "I guess I can," I said. "Yeah, I'll try and figure out a time."

I was mad at myself. I knew I couldn't and wouldn't find any time to help Janella. Why hadn't I said that? Next time she asked that I'd tell her I just didn't have time.

A day later, something else happened that was just as upsetting. I had become friends with a white guy named Jason. We were walking down the hall together when three black students stopped us. They asked both of us to be on their intramural basketball team. I wanted to play intramural and I wanted to be on a team with Jason. We had even talked about it. Jason told them yes, but I said that I wouldn't have time for intramurals. I wanted badly to play, but somehow I didn't want to play with black guys.

At my last school, I enjoyed singing in the choir. I have a good baritone voice. In the choral class here three blacks also have fine voices. The choral teacher, Mr. Curran, told the four of us that he was thinking about using us as a quartet for some numbers. No way! The next day I told Mr. Curran that I thought he should pick someone else. He must have guessed why. He asked me to give it some more thought.

"Did the quartet start practicing?" Jason asked on the way home that day.

"Looks now like it may not happen," I answered.

"Too bad," he commented. "It sounded like a good idea."

For the next week or so, I spent an hour or more in bed each night thinking that I was only hurting myself. Each night I became more upset with myself because I was losing chances to be involved in activities I liked. In the dark it made sense to share these activities with black students. Then at school the next day, it didn't make sense at all. I felt that same uneasiness again and I just couldn't do it.

I finally decided to tell Jason about my problem with black students. He listened quietly. "I figured there was something," he said.

"Yeah, there's something all right," I declared. "What am I going to do about it?"

"Hey, I'm no shrink. I don't know how to change people!"

"I know, Jason," I tried to assure him, "but you get along great with everybody."

He stared at me for just a moment. "Okay, I'll think about it," he conceded.

The next evening Jason rode over on his bike. "You wanted my help," Jason reminded me.

"That's right," I agreed.

"Okay, here it is. I think you should do three things—just keep doing them every day."

He waited. "What are they?" I asked.

"First, I want you to join our intramural team. It may be tough, but you have to do it and keep doing it," he stated firmly, watching my face. "You want to hear the second one?"

My agreement sounded weak even to me.

"You go back to Mr. Curran and tell him you want the quartet to happen and you want to be part of it. You do it and you keep doing it. Are you still with me?"

"I'm still listening," I answered.

"Finally, you find time to help Janella with her math. You do it and keep doing it."

Jason leaned closer to me. "You do those three things," he stressed. "Don't worry about anything else. Just those three things and stick to them. That's my help and I think it will work."

Shaping Strategies

1) Would Lyle overcome his resistance to black people without help?

2) What does Lyle's attitude cost him? What do you think it costs the black students?

3) If you were a schoolmate of Lyle's, how might you know he is having a problem?

4) Do you think Mr. Curran has guessed Lyle's problem? Has he tried to help? How?

5) Is Jason's idea a good helping effort? Why?

Putting Yourself in the Story

If you were Jason, what would you do next?

'It's Not Right!'

My real name is Martha, but everybody calls me Marty. Mary Jo
and I started kindergarten on the same day and soon discovered
that we were born on the same day. That made us better friends
each year as we celebrated our birthday together. When we got
to be 16 we kept right on doing things together.

My father needed two bus girls in his restaurant, one of the
biggest in town. He asked me if I wanted to work. I did, and when
he asked me to suggest a second person, I thought of Mary Jo. She
was really excited.

"Oh, I would like a job," she declared. "There are so many
things that I'd like to have my own money for!"

We both laughed about going to work on the same day. The
job was hard sometimes when things got busy. We used carts so
we didn't have anything really heavy to lift.

Everything was fine for two weeks. Then the envelopes with
our paychecks showed up at the cashier's table. Employees got
them when they finished their shift. Mary Jo and I worked the
same hours that day, so we picked up our envelopes together.

"Now we even get paid at the same time," Mary Jo laughed.

We went to the restroom before starting for home. I ripped
my envelope open and looked at the check. Mary Jo carefully
peeled hers open—she always was the tidy one.

"Hey, not bad," I chuckled. "A whole $63.90!"

Mary Jo stared at me. A moment later, she asked to repeat
what I had said. When I repeated it, she got a strange look on her
face. "Is there a mistake?" she asked, handing me her check. It
was made out for $34.50.

We had worked exactly the same hours. I could see that Mary
Jo was hurt. I would have been, too. My father had signed both
checks and I just did not understand.

"Should I ask somebody?" Mary Jo inquired.

"Tell you what. Let me ask about it," I told her.

Dad was off that night so I waited to talk to him at home. He
and Mom came in early from a visit to some of their friends. It
seemed strange to bring up the problem, but I wanted to know

and was sure Mary Jo had to know. To get started, I told about how we had opened our checks and what we had found.

"Yeah, that's right," Dad stated.

"That's just the point, Dad. It's not right," I protested.

"I don't understand," he said.

"I don't understand either. Why weren't we paid the same? We started at the same time and we did the same job for the same amount of time."

"But you're my daughter," he declared.

"I know that. What isn't fair is that Mary Jo got paid less than I did."

My father shrugged and smiled. "Do you want to work for what Mary Jo gets?" he asked.

"That wouldn't be fair either. You'd be cutting me back after paying me more," I argued.

"Well, I'm paying Mary Jo what I usually pay bus help. Of course, she gets something from the waitresses as a share of tips."

"We're both supposed to get something. They're very, very stingy! I think you ought to check into that."

My father took a deep breath and sighed. "I have a good set of waitresses, Marty, and I can't afford to lose any of them."

I was so frustrated that I just turned and ran upstairs to my room. Next evening at work, I explained to Mary Jo that he thought it was fair to pay his daughter more and I offered to split the differences in our checks. She wouldn't let me do that.

About an hour later the young man from the self-service gasoline station down the street came in with a date. We always bought candy and pop from him. He stopped me as I was passing his table. "Marty, how old are you?" he asked.

"Sixteen," I answered.

"Listen, I'm leaving for college. I'd be glad to speak to the boss about you taking my place."

I applied for the job and got it and my father was furious.

"Look, Dad, I'll get almost what you're paying me," I explained. "Also, I'll get a few more hours."

"I need you here!" he snapped.

"Hey, Dad, come on! You can hire two new girls for what you're paying me." It was his turn to be frustrated. He walked out, too.

The duties on my new job were interesting. My boss was very helpful during my training period. Twice in the first two weeks, he told me that I was doing a good job. Then he put me right in the center of a dilemma.

"Marty, I'm going to have another part-time position opening soon. Will you look around and see if you can spot a young person to recommend?"

"Sure, I'll be glad to," I told him.

Mary Jo was a natural person for the spot. That meant that she would be able to make much more than at the restaurant. It also meant that I would be hurting my father. For a whole day my mind kept coming back to the problem. That night I had a movie date. When I came in, there sat my father in his big chair with the evening paper. I knew I had to tell him before I talked to Mary Jo.

"Dad, I need to talk to you," I said.

"Okay," he replied, dropping his paper on the floor.

As carefully as I could, I told him about my predicament. That twinkle came to his eyes, the one I had learned as a little girl meant he was about to tease me.

"Help Mary Jo? What about your father?" he asked. Then he pulled me down and hugged me. "Go ahead and talk to her," he said.

Shaping Strategies

1) How would having a boss other than her father simplify the ways Marty could help Mary Jo?

2) Is there a danger that Marty might help Mary Jo at her father's expense? How should she handle this?

3) How is Marty helpful to Mary Jo?

4) Does Mary Jo appear to be a helpful person? Explain.

5) Is Marty's father trying to be helpful to Mary Jo? Explain.

Putting Yourself in the Story

If you were Marty, how would you have tried to help Mary Jo?

Just for Laughs

It was early when Dean and I got out of the movie. We walked along the street talking about it. Dean wasn't impressed by it. He thought most movies were pretty fake. "Come on, Matt," he said. "I'll take you to a real show!"

Dean led the way to an apartment house. He guided us through the shrubs alongside the building until we were opposite a lighted apartment. The drapes were open. Dean held up his hand in a signal for me to stop. He put his finger to his lips. As I looked in the window I saw a young woman undressing. We stood there until she turned out the light. Dean waved his arm and we left.

"Why did we do that?" I asked him. "I feel like a Peeping Tom."

"Come on!" Dean laughed. "I think it's funny. I watch her all the time."

My shades were down when I undressed and slipped into my pajamas. It was hard to fall asleep. I decided that Dean needed help. I had no idea how I was going to help him, but it seemed obvious that I had to try. I made up my mind to go see the school counselor and fell asleep.

"So that's what happened," I told the counselor. "I don't know what to do."

The counselor looked at me in silence for a minute. "You aren't looking for help for yourself, are you?" he inquired.

The question startled me for a moment. "No, I really do have a friend," I responded.

"Then whoever this guy is, you have to turn him in," he stated abruptly.

"I want to help him, not rat on him," I explained.

"He needs professional help," continued the counselor. "I'll see him. If I can't help him, I can refer him to someone who can."

"There has to be a better way," I objected. "I can't turn him in."

I saw Dean at our first home football game. He climbed the bleachers and sat down next to me. We were on the edge of the student section and we cheered now and then. Most of the time we talked. "Do you look in people's windows a lot?" I asked him.

"Not *every* night, but I like to look."

"Dean, you've got to stop," I argued. "It's sick!"

"People show off. I just look," he quipped.

"But looking is what's wrong."

"Aw, come on," he joked. "I just look for the laughs."

"Dean, this isn't funny."

At half-time he went to the refreshment stand and then disappeared. As I watched the second half, I knew that he was making the rounds of the neighborhood, looking into windows.

At that moment, I think I could have turned Dean in. I didn't feel like going out after the game. I walked home alone.

The next day was Saturday, a sunny day in early fall. I did some chores and errands for my mom in the morning. In the afternoon, I sat on the lawn in the sun with my portable radio. When I looked across the yard, I noticed that Mr. Mead, our neighbor, was down on his knees working on his flower beds. I'd seen his picture in the paper during the week. He had gotten the Mayor's Award as Police Officer of the Month.

I had always liked Mr. Mead. He and my dad had taken me hunting and fishing since I was a little boy. I walked over to him.

"Hi, Matt," he said as he smiled up at me.

I returned his hello and asked if I could talk to him. He rolled from his knees to the seat of his pants. "Sit down," he invited.

As we sat facing each other, I told him all about Dean, including the counselor's insistence that I should give him my friend's name. Mr. Mead listened very closely.

"You want to know how to help him?" he asked me.

"Yeah. I just can't figure out the right thing to do."

"You really don't want to turn him in, do you?" he questioned again.

"No. Well, I don't know. I want to help him, but I...don't know what to do."

"Do you want my help?" he inquired softly.

"Yes. Well, maybe. You tell me—do I?"

He smiled. "You've been wrestling with a tough decision, haven't you?"

"The toughest I've ever had," I replied.

"Okay, let me tell you what I can do. You tell me who he is and where he lives. That's all you have to do. Then you forget it.

I promise to see that he gets the right kind of help."

"What will you do?" I inquired.

"Matt, I'm a police officer. I have to handle this a police officer's way. I do promise to help your friend."

I realized that I had trusted this man all my life. I knew I could still trust him. I gave him Dean's name and address. As the next days passed, I continued to feel uneasy.

Two weeks had gone by when I saw the headline in the morning paper: "Peeping Tom Arrested." The offender's name wasn't given because he was a juvenile. They had watched him and caught him in the act three times. Then they arrested him. It had to be Dean.

"How will I ever help him now?" I asked myself again and again.

Shaping Strategies

1) Does what Mr. Mead did strike you as a good effort to help? Explain your answer.

2) Do you think that perhaps Matt misunderstood Mr. Mead? How?

3) Was the counselor prepared to help Dean? Explain.

4) Should Matt have turned Dean in as the counselor suggested? Why or why not?

5) How are the counselor and Mr. Mead different in Matt's eyes? Why did Matt choose to reveal Dean's identity to Mr. Mead?

Putting Yourself in the Story

If you were Matt, how would you feel about having tried to help Dean?

The Budding Writer

For people who love to write, words are fun. It has always been challenging for me just to play with words. I have always had a hunger to write, and my gratitude to my eighth-grade English teacher will last a lifetime. She pushed and pushed to make us write.

Once, Miss Gilliam assigned us an original 20-line poem. A lot of people were groaning, but for me it would be a simple job. That is, it was simple until my friends complicated it.

Hugh was the first one to come to me. "Julie, there is no way I can ever do that assignment," he said. "If I work for a hundred years, I won't have a poem."

I agreed to write his poem for him. He told somebody who told somebody else, and the word got out. It started a flood. I ended up writing 16 poems in all.

We all handed them in. I had kept what I thought was the best one for myself. When they came back with comments and grades on them, I got a C. Four of the poems I wrote for my friends got A's and seven got B's. At first, I felt sick. Then I was angry, very angry. If this is what you get for helping your friends, then I wasn't helping anybody ever again.

That grade was bad enough. What followed was even worse. My classmates began coming around asking how they could help or make me feel better or something. Hugh, who got one of the A's, wanted to confess the whole thing.

"You can't do that," I told him. "You'll get everybody in trouble!"

Barb wanted to know how she could make me feel better. Daphne apologized. Almost all of the 15 wanted me to tell them how to help me. I kept saying they should forget it, but I couldn't forget my C. I never got C's in literature or writing.

Miss Gilliam topped everything. She called me in and told me how impressed she had been all term with my writing. I was so pleased I wanted to challenge the grade on the poem, but I chickened out.

"Would you be interested in going to school one night each

week?" she asked me.

At first, I didn't even understand what her question meant. "What for?" I asked. "I go all day."

"I know that!" she declared a bit impatiently. "An old friend of mine is a well-established author. She is offering a special evening class for adults interested in writing short stories. The ordinary rule is that you have to be 18 to take these classes."

"That lets me out," I interrupted. "I'm two years short."

She gave me that "poor dumb child" look she uses from time to time. "No matter," she answered crisply. "My friend assures me she will make an exception if I recommend you."

I finally realized that Miss Gilliam was serious about that night class for me. "Are you interested?" she asked.

"What do I have to do?"

"Tell me you are interested," she responded. "In this case, 'interested' means you agree to stay with the class every session and work hard."

"Well, it's writing," I began thinking aloud. "Anything that involves writing interests me."

"I'll call her right away," she concluded. "I'm going to call your parents also so I can explain this to them."

The first night I walked timidly into the classroom and sat quickly in the first empty desk. The author-teacher followed me in and almost immediately had each of us stand to tell something about ourselves. Most of those adults were clever, humorous and had lots of experience. When my turn came, I was still trying to decide what to say. I stood and glanced quickly at the people in the room with me. What I said just slipped out.

"I am Julie and I escaped from a high school," I reported. Everyone chuckled as I sat down.

I was the youngest in the class. Mr. Kelly was the oldest at 68. In between us were 18 would-be writers. It was really a bit frightening for me, especially when we began criticizing each other's stories. If Miss Gilliam thought she was helping me, that beginning was worse than a C.

"When you come to class," our instructor advised, "be sure you are wearing your thickest skin. We will be as honest as we can. Listen to what your classmates say about what you write. They are an important part of the reading audience."

Gradually I got used to the criticism. One lady never did. When I told her that her story lacked a strong plot, she cried. When I got home, I cried. I was only trying to help her.

The author-teacher became very stern at times. "If you can't take criticism, don't try to write," she would say. "If you ask for criticism and the person says 'Oh, it's very nice,' and nothing else, then throw the piece away. Your critic has just said that it is worthless."

She didn't know it, but these proclamations made it possible for me to stay and take the criticism and the praise. They also made it important for me to evaluate my classmates seriously. She'll never know how much she helped me.

Shaping Strategies

1) Was Julie's writing poems for classmates a good effort to help? Explain.

2) Was Miss Gilliam's arranging for Julie to attend the adult class a good effort to help? Why?

3) What helpful techniques did the author-teacher use?

4) Julie was angry enough about the C to think she would not help anyone again. Do you agree or disagree with that idea? Why?

5) If Miss Gilliam knew that Julie wrote the 16 poems, could giving Julie a C be a way of helping? Explain.

Putting Yourself in the Story

If you were Julie, would you see yourself as a helpful person?

A Little Project

Dad's company transferred him to San Francisco. I had to leave some really great friends. It was tougher because we had just started a little project.

Holly has a great voice and often accompanied herself with her guitar. She was really good. She had filled in late in the summer as the featured singer at the county fair. She has performed at many weddings. On weekends she's been singing with a popular jazz combo. She was always bright and happy. Just one thing bothered her: She had herself psyched out. She was convinced that she could not do well in anything but music.

I didn't tell you my name. It's Justin. I'm a whiz in science but, like everybody else, I have my down areas—like English.

One day our science teacher had given us some class study time. "Why can't I learn these stupid terms in biology?" Holly whispered to me. She was smart enough to learn them. She just kept telling herself she wasn't.

"Yeah, and why can't I sing two notes in a row?" I whispered back.

She got an F on one math test. "I wish I could do something besides music," she complained. "I had a B up to now. This made that into a C."

Kelly replied, "Come on, don't run yourself down all the time."

Jonathan helped her with one of the problems on the math homework assignment. She thanked him. "It sure would be fantastic to be able to do math the way you do," she added.

"You're really better at math than you think," Jonathan assured her.

Then the first report cards came out. "Typical," declared Holly. "A in music and C in everything else. Even the C's are because all the teachers like me." She laughed.

"That's no joke," Janet scolded her. "Everybody likes you!"

"I know, and I like everybody," Holly agreed with a smile. "I just wish that I wasn't so dumb."

That did it. I was getting completely frustrated with her attitude. Everyone told her she wasn't dumb, but she kept telling herself that she was. I was sure that if Holly quit being so negative, she would get better grades.

The next week it happened again. I overheard her talking to Carla, who is probably her best friend. "There! I did it again," she complained. "Another D on a history test."

Carla's first reply was a little grunt. Then she spoke. "So move over," she said. "I got one, too."

I invited Carla to go to the pizza parlor with me. I could hardly wait to tell her what was on my mind. "Carla, how do you help someone who really has ability but has convinced herself that she does not have?" I asked.

"You must mean Holly!" she guessed.

I just nodded.

"I've been thinking about her, too," Carla added. "What do you think we can do?"

"I have an idea. It may not work."

"Tell me," she suggested.

"Suppose we all find chances to ask Holly for help of some kind with our work. I can't ask her for help in biology, but I can in English. You can't ask in English. You're too good there. You might in history."

Carla grinned brightly. "You think every time she helps one of us, it will erase some of her negative attitude about herself?"

"What do you think?"

"I'd like to try it! We could get some other people to work on it, too. If she helps enough of us, she'll just have to change her mind. It'll be fun convincing her that she's not as dumb as she thinks."

Carla agreed to line up seven or eight others who would be part of our plan. We gave ourselves a week to get it all in gear. We knew we couldn't be too obvious. On the other hand, Carla was excited and eager to help her best friend.

At home that very night, when we sat down to dinner, Dad told us about his transfer. He had just a hint of the possibility about a week earlier but decided to wait until it really developed before saying anything. It was final and it meant we would move very quickly. The company had already found a house for us to move to temporarily. Dad's boss had made arrangements to take over selling ours. The day our project to help Holly was to kick off, I was saying good-bye to all my friends.

Carla had things all lined up. Still excited about convincing Holly she had ability, she grumbled about my going away. "Why don't you move in with one of us and stay for a month or two?" she asked.

"I can't do that. Our family goes where Dad goes."

"It was your idea. I wish you could be here," she pouted.

"You send me an address and I'll keep you posted."

Shaping Strategies

1) Was the friends' "project" a good effort to help? Why or why not?

2) Is Justin genuinely interested in being a helper? Explain.

3) Is Carla's leadership apt to bring success in helping Holly? Why?

4) How would you answer Justin's question: "How do you help someone who really has ability but has convinced herself that she does not have?" Explain your answer.

5) Would it be easier to help Holly, who is bright, happy and popular, than someone who is sullen and gloomy? Why?

Putting Yourself in the Story

If you were Justin, would you feel cheated by having to leave now? Why?

'It's Too Hard!'

My name is Juanita. My happiest place is at home where my sisters and brothers make me laugh. My father got his citizenship a year ago. Before that our whole family were migrant workers. We followed crops almost all year. After he was a citizen, my dad got a job here in one of the plants. We don't travel anymore.

Last year I went all year to the same school for the first time in my life. I was 15 and in my sophomore year. I wasn't a very good student and I had almost no friends. Just one girl, Wanda, always talked to me last year. We were in the same science class and did our lab together. She was very smart and she helped me to like science.

When we started school this year, I watched for Wanda so we could talk again. I saw her coming. She walked up the walk toward the bench where I was sitting.

"Hi, Juanita," Wanda said to me.

"Hello, Wanda," I answered.

"How was your summer?" she asked. I told her I'd had a wonderful summer. It was the first summer when I did not work in the farm fields. We talked about our schedules. We did not have any classes together and that disappointed me.

"Oh, I'll see you every day anyway," laughed Wanda.

I knew she meant it. We did meet almost every day, sometimes just to talk for a minute, sometimes to eat lunch together.

"It's impossible to make any friends," I told Wanda one day. "So far, you're the only one."

"I have an idea," Wanda said. "You come over any night you can. I'll teach you how to fix your hair in a lot of different styles. Maybe a new hairstyle will make you feel more confident and you'll find it easier to make friends."

When I went to her house, she showed me how to do different things with my hair. She had just gotten a new set of curlers for her birthday, so she gave me her old set. My hair got prettier but my grades got worse, especially in English.

"If we ask your English teacher, she'll get you a peer tutor," Wanda suggested. "You need to learn to speak English better before you can read or write it."

The tutor did help my English get better, but I still had a lot of problems in class.

One day I came to school with a cast on my right hand. "What happened?" Wanda asked when she saw me in the hall.

"I broke my wrist in PE yesterday. Mrs. Carson even called me a clod!"

"How did you do it?"

I explained how we were all running laps at the end of the class. Somehow I tripped and fell on my wrist. It was badly hurt. The doctor said it would be a long time before the cast could come off.

"Why did Mrs. Carson call you a clod?"

I laughed.

"She said not very many people manage to smash a wrist running laps," I answered.

Wanda laughed with me. I really liked her. She always stopped to talk about how things were going for me. She took time to eat lunch with me every week. She was into every activity in school, but she was still my friend. I wished I was as smart as she was. She learned everything so quickly. She was always giving me pep talks.

"You're getting better in English," she told me. "I can tell. You're prettier when you fix your hair. You have more friends than you used to have. Keep fighting, Nita!"

"Yeah, but how am I going to do my homework when I can't write?" I asked her. "I can't even fix my hair with one hand!"

I kept having problems with my grades. I was never very smart in school and even though I worked hard, my grades always stayed low. It was frustrating. Wanda noticed, as she always did.

"You seem down these days," she observed. "What's wrong?"

"Oh, I think it would be easier to just work in a restaurant or something. Maybe I could get on at the factory making boxes."

"Sure, but you'll always work for nothing and only when there's work," Wanda declared firmly. "Stick it out here at school! You can do better that way."

She talked me into it. I did my best to keep going to my classes at school. After a few weeks, the doctor took off the cast and I learned how to use my right hand again. All the time I kept getting more and more convinced that school was not the place for me. The one bright spot was Wanda, who always had lunch with me once a week.

"Wanda, I'm going to drop out," I told her. "School just is never going to be for me."

"Hey, wait a minute! We have to talk about this," she reacted immediately. I knew she would not want me to do it. For several months, she had kept convincing me to stay.

"We've talked many times, Wanda," I answered her. "I'm sorry. I know you think I should stay in school but I just don't like it. It's too hard. I'm going to quit."

Shaping Strategies

1) Has Wanda made a good effort to help Juanita? Explain.

2) Should Wanda try to help Juanita stay in school when she really doesn't want to? Why?

3) Should Wanda enlist the aid of others to get Juanita to stay in school? What others?

4) What might be done to encourage Juanita to stay in school?

5) What obstacles lead a person to think about dropping out of school? Can other teens help in overcoming these obstacles? Explain.

Putting Yourself in the Story

If you were Wanda, what would you do next?

PART FOUR

Taking Time

Situations and people seldom change immediately. Helping takes time—sometimes a long time. Sometimes, in fact, we *never* see the fruit of our effort.

The stories in this section present teens involved in a helping situation over a period of time. Their purpose is to help young people realize that helping relationships are more like motion pictures than like snapshots, involving a series of contacts between the helper and the person being helped. An individual who has truly developed a strong helpful attitude will likely devote much time to assisting others. Young people need to learn that deep and continuing satisfactions grow out of being a helper.

The stories in this section are designed to help teens consider the following points:

- how long a helping relationship may last;

- some reasons why helping may take time;

- whether or not we should try to estimate how long helping might take;

- why a helper might let helping drag on.

First Girl

The three sophomores had been close friends for over four years. Chuck and Pete dated a lot of different girls; Gary had yet to ask a girl out. When girls joined the group, Gary usually stayed home.

One November afternoon Chuck, Pete and Gary sat on the bench outside the neighborhood branch library, where they had been researching a social studies report.

"Why are you so grumpy today?" Pete asked Gary.

"I'm not grumpy," Gary protested.

"Yeah, you are. I've noticed it, too," Chuck observed.

Gary stared at the book in his lap. "Well, I think I'd like to ask Wendy out," he told his friends.

Chuck and Pete smiled. "And that makes you grumpy?" asked Chuck.

"Not exactly," Gary replied. "She just won't pay any attention to me."

The next day Pete and Chuck waved their "I'll see you" to Gary as he turned up his street on their way home from school. Gary hadn't said any more about Wendy. After they had walked a block in silence, Pete spoke. "Why don't we help old Gary out?" he asked.

"How?"

"Let's talk to Wendy."

"I don't know what we'd say," Chuck confessed.

"Neither do I, but we can still talk to her," Pete continued. "We'll think of something."

After school the next day, Pete and Chuck slipped away from Gary. They found Wendy in the band room practicing her flute. Pete walked up to her. "We'd like to talk to you when you're through practicing," he explained. "We can wait outside."

"Oh, I can talk now. I really don't have much to practice."

Pete and Chuck paused, then looked at each other. "Okay, I'll tell her," Chuck conceded. "We want to talk about Gary. You know who he is?"

"Yes," Wendy responded cautiously.

"Well, Gary really likes you and...."

"You must be kidding," she interrupted, her face reddening. She grabbed her flute. "I think I'd better practice," she added.

That Friday the three boys walked home together as they usually did. Chuck and Pete had decided not to tell Gary about their attempted help.

"You still down in the dumps?" Pete asked Gary.

"I shouldn't have told you guys," Gary answered.

"Sure you should. We're your friends," Chuck declared. Gary grunted.

"So you're still grouching about Wendy," Pete insisted.

"I don't want to talk about it," Gary said with unmistakable firmness.

The next week Chuck and Pete were shopping for a new cassette when Wendy entered the record department. She walked to the special order counter. Pete watched for a moment and then followed her.

"Hi, Wendy," he greeted her from behind.

She turned quickly. "Oh, hello, Pete," she said.

"Listen, don't get angry with me," Pete cautioned. "We didn't mean to embarrass you the other day. We just wanted to tell you that Gary likes you and he thinks you don't pay any attention to him."

"So now you've told me." She started to turn away, then turned to face Pete and Chuck, smiling and calm. "Hey, guys, I'm sorry to sound nasty, but why don't you let him talk to me himself?"

The next afternoon Gary faced a pair of aggressive friends as they walked home. "Gary," Pete began, "have you ever *tried* to talk to Wendy?"

"Well, no, not exactly," Gary replied.

"Then why do you complain that she doesn't pay attention to you?" Chuck demanded.

"Hey, what's with you guys?" asked Gary.

"No. What's with you? Don't you come grumbling around us until you find the nerve to go talk to Wendy yourself," advised Pete.

"Yeah, for all you know she may be expecting you to talk to her," Chuck added.

The next week, Gary gave it a try. "Wendy, I'm Gary," he began.

"Yes, I know," Wendy acknowledged.

With that, Gary stopped and stood silent for a full minute. When she could hold in no longer, Wendy burst into a happy laugh. "Hey, Gary, I don't bite," she giggled.

"Oh, I didn't think you did," Gary assured her. "I was having a hard time deciding what to say."

She laughed again. "Is it bashfulness or a small vocabulary?" she needled him.

"No. No. Neither of those," he replied softly. "It's you." Without another word, he turned and walked—almost ran—away from her.

All Gary told his friends was that he had talked to Wendy. "Yes, I talked to her," he repeated. "But I got nowhere. I guess I'll just give up any idea that she's going to pay any attention to me."

Taking Time

1) What are some ways Chuck and Pete tried to help Gary?

2) Would you want to receive such help from your friends? Explain.

3) Are there any ways his friends might help Gary to help himself?

4) Why don't Chuck and Pete let Gary know how they are trying to help?

5) Could Wendy be more helpful? How? Should she be?

Putting Yourself in the Story

If you were Chuck or Pete, what would you do next?

Double Trouble

Tara came to Orchard High School to begin her sophomore year when her father was transferred from another state. The third week of school, the physical education class started playing soccer. Mrs. Marks had used a wide variety of activities up to then.

The first day they practiced skills and learned some of the rules. Gail was working in the same group as Tara. They were on opposite teams. Gail raced the ball down the field. She had just made the kick for a goal when she saw Tara. The ball came off the ground and hit Tara full in the face. Tara went sprawling. Gail ran to retrieve the ball. Mrs. Marks blew her whistle.

"Time's up. Everybody in," she shouted.

The teacher hurried to check Tara. Gail ran with the others to the locker room.

The next morning Gail saw Tara in the hall. She went to her immediately.

As she faced Tara she could see how badly she was injured. Tara's lips were swollen and she had two black eyes. When Tara tried to smile, her expression showed that it still hurt. "Hey, I'm sorry. I didn't mean to kick the ball in your face," Gail said.

"Don't worry about it. I always have a hard time in any fast activity, especially with balls," Tara explained. "I see everything double—like a permanent drunk. You only hit me with one ball, but I saw two. It's tough to know which one to dodge."

During PE that afternoon, Gail kept watching Tara. She could see that Tara was very badly coordinated. Her arms and legs went in all directions when she tried to run. She kicked at the ball but seldom hit it. When one of the girls threw Tara the ball, she made a clumsy grab for it.

Gail and Tara ate lunch together that Friday. "You said you see everything double. Don't your glasses help?" Gail asked.

"Just a little bit—almost not at all," Tara answered.

"Can't some doctor do something?"

"My dad's had several look at me. They all say I'll have to learn to live with my eyes the way they are," Tara reported with a little shrug.

"What do you mean—learn?"

"They say I should be as active as I can. By working at it, I'll maybe adjust to the problem. I may get a little better that way," Tara replied.

Gail studied Tara's face. The swelling was almost gone and black was turning purple and green. "Listen, I have an idea. You want to be active. Could we work out together?"

On Saturday Tara met Gail in the park. Gail had brought a large whiffle ball. She taught Tara the stretching exercises she used before running. After they did them together, they played catch with the ball. Tara soon learned that she could get hit with the whiffle ball without getting hurt. She worked hard but achieved little success catching the ball.

On Monday morning, Gail went to see Mrs. Marks before school. She told her about Saturday.

"Will Tara ever improve?" asked Gail.

"I don't know for sure. I've talked to her parents. They want Tara to participate as much as possible. They're all accepting things as they are."

"I won't hurt her by working out with her?" Gail asked.

"Not if you can stand it," the teacher grinned. "You are a talented athlete; you work seriously at becoming really good. Tara can never begin to keep up with you."

After Gail and Tara completed their sixth Saturday workout together, they agreed that there had been a slight gain in Tara's ability to catch and run. Gail went with Tara to talk to the doctor. He encouraged them to continue their shared activity. He advised Tara that progress would be slow but important.

Then Tara took a fall during a workout and broke her left arm. Gail was discouraged by the accident. Over lunch the following Monday she told Tara that maybe they should quit. Tara said nothing for a long time. Then she spoke.

"Look, Gail, I know I can't do much. I'm as clumsy as anyone ever was. If you want to quit, I'll understand. I have to say thank you. You've done a lot for me!"

Taking Time

1) What are some of the ways Gail has tried to help Tara? Was she successful?

2) Will attempting to help Tara bring quick success? Why should Gail try?

3) Would Gail better spend her time developing her own athletic talent? Why or why not?

4) How will Gail know whether or not she is really helping Tara?

5) Gail seeks advice from Mrs. Marks and from Tara's doctor. Is that a good idea? Why?

Putting Yourself in the Story

If you were Gail, what would you do next?

Home Alone

When Keith's father was sent to Europe for a month, his mother decided to go along. That left Keith at home alone, but his parents decided he would be able to take care of himself. He was a sophomore, an honor student and usually a reliable person. Besides, they were uneasy about leaving the house empty. They gave Keith a list of people he could call if he needed anything.

Soon after they left, Keith visited his friend Bart. He invited Bart to spend some weekends with him.

"Sure. Maybe one or two," Bart replied. "You must get lonely in that house. What can we do with a weekend?"

Keith laughed. "I get excited even thinking about the possibilities," he answered. "We can get some girls out to play strip poker or take showers with us...."

Bart frowned. "Not funny," he said. "Bad joke!"

"Hey, I'm not joking!" Keith protested. "I got a house all to myself. I'm going to have fun."

"Listen, buddy, it looks like you're going to need lots of help to get through this month," observed Bart. "You don't want to do stuff like that."

"You don't think so? I think I have the opportunity of a lifetime."

"Think about it," Bart suggested. "And then don't do it."

A few days later Bart and Mike sat together in the high school cafeteria, trying to work out a math problem. Keith joined them.

"Hi, what you guys doing?" he asked.

They told him. "Let's see. Oh, you're almost there. Just divide both sides of the equation by this and you can solve it."

"OK, brain," Mike smiled. "Thanks."

Keith bent close to the table. "You should have accepted my invite, Bart."

"Oh, so what happened?"

Keith grinned smugly. "Susie spent all Saturday afternoon with me," he reported. "Yes, sir! We played. Nothing heavy. A shower together was the highlight. And Joanie was over for a poker game on Sunday."

Mike look puzzled; Bart scowled at his friend. "Okay, dummy," he snapped. "You did it. Now grow up."

"Oh, I am growing up," Keith argued. "That's what it's all about. I am growing up!"

"No, you're not," Bart shot back. "You're acting like a jerk."

For a week after Bart and Keith clashed, they went through a cooling-off period. Then one day Keith found Bart eating his lunch alone. "Can I sit down or are you still mad at me?" he asked.

Bart pulled out a chair. "Sure, sit down. And I wasn't mad at you. I just can't figure you out."

"Don't worry about me, friend. I have everything figured out," Keith assured him.

Bart raised his eyebrows.

"All right. Let me tell you," offered Keith. "You did make me realize that all weekend was too much. But I have to use my house all I can. I worked out a plan to have just one celebration per weekend. That's only four times while my parents are gone."

Bart held his head in frustration. "Keith, how can I get through to you? You're hurting every girl you use this way."

"They're having fun!"

"They play your games with you. Then you dump each one to go after someone else. That's not nice and it's not fair."

The following week, Bart met Mike in the hall right after afternoon dismissal. Mike's face wore an unhappy frown and he walked very slowly.

"Hey, you look down," Bart observed. "You wanta talk about it?"

"Not here. Let's go get something to drink."

Once they were settled into the privacy of a booth, Mike stared at Bart. "Well, our friend did it again," he stated. "Janet spent Saturday afternoon with him."

"Did he tell you?"

"No, Janet did. And you know how I feel about her," Mike said.

Bart nodded.

"What makes a girl do a dumb thing like that?" asked Mike.

"Keith is big, good-looking and very popular. What's more, he's still playing the field," Bart said.

Keith and Bart had slipped into a silent agreement that their

111

conversations would not include Keith's activities. But the next Monday, as they sat in the back of the math classroom waiting for the bell, Keith asked, "Who's the most popular sophomore girl?"

"I don't know. Maybe Paula."

"Bingo!" exclaimed Keith. "She was at my place Saturday."

Bart said nothing. But at lunch he cornered Keith in the cafeteria. "Keith, you've been my best friend all through school. I just don't know you anymore. I don't know what's happened to you."

"So what do you want me to do?" Keith asked.

"Don't play dumb. You can't feel great about what you're doing. You're moving girls in and out of that house like pieces of furniture," Bart said.

"What's wrong with it?" Keith shrugged. "They can say no. The rules are simple: no screwing, no pregnancy, no trouble."

"Oh, great! You're getting to be just like my dog. He runs down the street from one bitch to another and another. That's what I meant when I said you were acting like an animal."

Bart sucked in some air.

"One last word, old buddy," Bart continued. "If I can't help you, I sure can help the girls. Once more and I go to every girl's parents. When yours get back, I go to them. Then you tell me your simple rules mean no trouble!"

Taking Time

1) Is Bart really attempting to help Keith? Explain.

2) What are some ways Bart and Mike might have tried to help Keith?

3) In the long run, will Bart's turning against Keith help Keith? How?

4) Why is Bart concerned about the girls? Do you agree with him? Why or why not?

5) What makes helping Keith difficult?

6) What sort of help do you think Keith really needs? Who might give that help?

Putting Yourself in the Story

If you were Bart, would you carry out your threat?

A Bed for Eduardo

Eduardo was tall and thin but wiry. He was very strong, as he proved in gym classes and in occasional horseplay with other students. Eduardo seemed to live in the same pair of jeans until they were worn out, but they were always clean.

Eduardo came from a very poor family. Sometimes he brought no lunch and he never had money to buy it.

"Eduardo, why don't you see the principal? He can get you a free lunch everyday," Carlos suggested.

"No," Eduardo stated emphatically.

"Hey, I can't blame you for not wanting to eat the food in the cafeteria! Here, eat one of my sandwiches." Carlos held out the plastic bag containing the sandwich. Eduardo hesitated.

"My mom always makes me two sandwiches," Carlos explained. "That was fine during football. Now it's too much."

Eduardo stared thoughtfully at Carlos. "I'd like to play football next season," he said quietly.

The next day Eduardo stood near the entrance to the cafeteria for a minute or two. Then he walked slowly to where Carlos was sitting with two other guys. "Can I sit with you?" he asked.

"Why not?" Carlos questioned back. "Sit down. Here, Eduardo, help me with this sandwich, will you?"

Eduardo immediately accepted the sandwich with a grateful smile.

The next weekend, Eduardo invited Carlos to his house. It was just before 10:00 when Carlos got there. He had a hard time finding it because neither the streets nor the houses in the neighborhood were well marked.

"I didn't think you'd come," Eduardo greeted him.

"You asked me and I accepted. Why wouldn't I come?"

"I've asked others who didn't come."

Carlos accepted that statement with an understanding grin and followed Eduardo into the house. He met Eduardo's mother and a roomful of brothers and sisters before going with his friend to a bedroom. Carlos scanned the room. The worn wooden floor was a dark mahogany color, giving the place a drab tone. The walls, last painted a long time ago, were a dingy green highlighted by several holes where the plaster had fallen away, exposing the wooden lath and studs. A bed occupied one side of the room while three smaller mats lined the floor on the other side.

"My little brothers sleep there," explained Eduardo, indicating the mats. "The bed is for me."

The following week, Carlos invited Eduardo to spend the night. Carlos took Eduardo upstairs to show him where he was to sleep: in the upper deck of the bunk bed. "I've never known why my mom put a double-decker in my room," Carlos pondered. "Now I know. It's for Eduardo."

Eduardo looked in awe at the large room with its carpeted floor and nice furniture. "Carlos, you live in a castle," he said. "Maybe we should not be friends. I haven't got a big house or much money or nice clothes."

Carlos reached out with a bear hug. "We'll be friends," he said.

The second semester began. Eduardo continued to "help" Carlos by eating the second sandwich. One day they were talking about their classes. "I want to do math and I want to do science, and to read and write. Mom has always told me how important school is," said Eduardo.

Carlos pushed three spiral notebooks across the table. "These are extras. I won't need them. Can you use them?"

Eduardo hesitated. "Don't do that to me," Carlos cautioned. "If you don't take them, some guy that'll waste them will end up taking them. You need spirals to do a good job of studying."

Almost affectionately, Eduardo gathered up the notebooks.

As the school year drew to a close, Eduardo and Carlos sat on the lawn, enjoying the warm, spring sun. "Eduardo, what are you going to do this summer?" inquired Carlos.

"I don't know. I have to find a good job if I'm going to play football next fall. It's really hard."

"I'll be working on my uncle's farm," Carlos reported. "He needs another worker. Do you want to go?"

"Sounds great!" Eduardo replied.

Eduardo worked hard and ate hard all summer. By the middle of August he was 30 pounds heavier than he had been in May. He was in great shape, ready to begin football practice. Carlos and Eduardo talked about football all through their last day of work on the farm. They couldn't wait for practice to begin.

"I can buy my shoes," Eduardo told Carlos, "but I wish I didn't have to pay that insurance fee."

"Listen, Scrooge, you haven't spent a penny all summer. What are you doing with your money?"

"I'm giving it to Mom," Eduardo responded.

Carlos slapped Eduardo on the shoulder. "You pay your insurance and give Mom the rest," he said.

Taking Time

1) How does Carlos help Eduardo?

2) Is it more difficult to help people who are "different"? Why or why not?

3) What do you think was Eduardo's greatest need for help? Explain.

4) What traits make Carlos a good helper?

5) Is Eduardo a helper? Explain.

Putting Yourself in the Story

If you were Carlos, what would you do next?

The Trilateral Trio

Now in their sophomore year, Brad, Evan and Mark had a classic friendship. For 10 years the three of them had attended the same schools, participated in the same summer activities and been inseparable companions.

Thanksgiving weekend Brad and Evan sat in Mark's basement family room. "We ought to have a name for us," Evan observed.

"You mean like the Three Musketeers?" asked Brad.

"Yeah, but something more original."

They looked at Mark, who shrugged his shoulders. They explored a lot of possibilities. "How about 'Trilateral Trio'?" Brad finally suggested.

"Don't laugh," cautioned Mark. "I like it."

"So do I," Evan concurred. The Trilateral Trio had been involved in many activities, but dating had never been one of them. It was almost on a dare that Brad asked Tanya for a date early in December. Tanya was probably the most popular girl in their class. None of the trio really expected that she would say yes to Brad. She always had all the dates she could ever want.

"She said *yes?*" Evan asked in disbelief.

"Forget about her," observed Mark. "Our buddy here is deserting us for a female! *That* surprises me."

At lunch a week later, Brad and Mark found Evan waiting at one of the cafeteria tables, a smug little grin on his face.

"Okay, tell us," Mark prompted.

"Tonight *I* have a date with Tanya," Evan reported with a cocky flourish.

"Another traitor!" exclaimed Mark.

"Not at all," Evan countered. "She talks to you all the time—a lot more than she does to either of us."

"Well, maybe," admitted Mark.

"How come you asked Tanya?" Brad inquired. "There's lots of other girls around."

"She doesn't belong to you, does she?" Evan shot back.

The next week it was again Brad's turn to boast about his date with Tanya. Evan reacted angrily. "So what if you do have a date with her? That's fine with me. I had fun on our date and I'll ask her again."

"I don't understand you," Brad answered. "There are plenty of others you can ask."

"So ask them!" returned Evan.

Mark broke in. "C'mon, guys, it's almost Christmas. Let's have a little peace on earth."

New Year's Day Brad and Evan met in front of Mark's home, where the Trio was going to watch bowl games. "You went out with Tanya twice during Christmas break," accused Brad.

"Sure, I did. So did you," Evan fired back.

"I dated her first. I want you to stop."

Evan laughed. "That's nuts! I won't stop and you can't stop me," he declared.

Brad's reply was a quick jab to Evan's forehead. Evan stepped back, a surprised look on his face. When Brad pursued, an all-out fight followed. Before Mark rushed out to stop them, Brad's nose was bleeding and Evan had a nasty gash on his chin from Brad's ring.

"I thought you guys were friends," Mark snapped.

The next Friday, Mark sat alone on a bleacher seat watching the basketball teams warm up for the first conference game. Normally he would have been with Brad and Evan, but the Trio had not been together since the fight.

"Is it all right if I sit here?" Mark turned to see Tanya standing beside him.

"Sure, sit down," he laughed.

They sat silently for a couple of minutes. Tanya spoke first. "Were Brad and Evan fighting over me?" she asked.

"Yes," Mark answered.

"I figured that was it," Tanya went on. "I told them both I won't date them anymore. Do you think I'm wrong?"

"No, I understand. I told them I wouldn't see either one of them alone. We're the Trilateral Trio or we're nobody," Mark reported.

"Hey, look, I feel like I destroyed the Trio!"

"Don't," advised Mark. "They did it."

"Is there something we can do to get them to make up?" Tanya inquired.

"I've been asking that, too," said Mark.

The next weekend Mark and Tanya met again at the basketball game. They sat together talking.

"Well, I talked to them," Mark reported. "Brad says he doesn't need Evan. Evan says Brad started it, so Brad has to make the first move. It looks like a standoff."

"Is there something we can do?" asked Tanya.

"Or should we even be trying to do anything?" Mark added.

Taking Time

1) Has the Trio broken up because its members have failed to help each other? Explain.

2) Tanya refuses to date either Brad or Evan. Is that helpful? Why or why not?

3) Mark said: "We're the Trilateral Trio or we're nobody." Why do you think he takes that position?

4) Mark questions whether he should even try to put the Trio back together. Is this a helpful stance? Explain.

5) Who is responsible for the breakup: Tanya, Brad, Evan or Mark? Why?

Putting Yourself in the Story

If you were Mark or Tanya, what would you do next?

Hard to Help

Crystal was still in the first semester of her freshman year at Carroll High School, but everybody knew she was trouble. "Crystal again?" was becoming a common question among teachers.

When the first freshman assembly was held in the auditorium, Crystal sat in an aisle seat three rows from the back. Her friend Ginger sat next to her. The activities director introduced the presentation. The program began and Crystal went to sleep. Ginger nudged her once but, when Crystal only squirmed, she let her sleep. At the end of the assembly, Ginger tugged roughly at Crystal's arm and she woke up.

As they walked from the auditorium, they passed the principal. "Crystal, that's the last time you sleep in school," she said quietly but firmly.

Crystal whirled toward the principal. "Did you see any whites asleep?" she snapped.

Ginger pushed her friend away. "Come on," she insisted. "We don't want to be late for class."

Early in October the English teacher passed back compositions. Crystal looked at the comments in the margins and raised her hand. "Would I have as many mistakes if I wasn't black?" she asked sarcastically.

The next morning Crystal walked to school with Ginger, who was still upset with her friend. "Why were you barking like a dog when the English teacher was only trying to help you?"

"She can keep her white help!" Crystal growled.

"Don't be dumb," Ginger added softly.

The next week Mr. Dunn returned algebra homework. His note to Crystal complimented her for doing all the problems. It also suggested that if Crystal would see him for a minute after class, Mr. Dunn would show her a shorter way to work the problems. Crystal stared at her paper for a few seconds before blurting out her question. "If my work is right, how come you're picking on me?" she asked.

As they walked home, Ginger looked at Crystal's math paper. She shook her head. "There you go again, Crystal. The man was only trying to help you. He just wants you to be better in math."

Crystal scowled but said nothing.

Soon after that, one of Crystal's teachers warned her to "get with it" in class.

"I do my homework. Don't you believe I do my own homework?" she challenged.

"Yes, Crystal," the teacher replied. "I know it's your work. It always has your kind of mistakes in it. I just want you to participate in class."

Crystal cupped her chin in her hands, planted her elbows on her desk and pouted for the rest of the period.

After school, the two friends sat on Ginger's front step, sharing the warm cookies they had just made.

"Why are you always making trouble? Nobody said you don't do your own homework. They're talking about your classwork." Ginger paused. "You know you just sit there like a lump."

In the lunchline the following week, Crystal saw the student ahead of her get a larger slice of roast beef. She turned back to Ginger. "See that?" she complained. "The white kid gets the big piece and I get the little piece."

"Yeah, and the next time you get the big piece," Ginger answered impatiently. "Here, I'll trade you. I got a big piece."

In PE that afternoon, Crystal clashed with a black teacher. Mrs. Matson spoke to Ginger later. "You're Crystal's friend," she said. "Can you tell me why it is so hard to work with her? I want to help her. She's got a good mind and she's a good athlete. Do you know what's bugging her?"

"No," Ginger replied. "Crystal is just a hard person to help."

Taking Time

1) How has Ginger tried to help Crystal?

2) Does Ginger give up even though Crystal frustrates her? What is good about Ginger's efforts?

3) If you were one of Crystal's teachers, would you try to help her? Explain.

4) Do you think just one helping can turn Crystal around? Why?

5) What do you think Ginger means when she says: "Crystal is just a hard person to help"?

Putting Yourself in the Story

If you were Ginger, what would you do next?

Guardian Angel

Greta's brother Kurt was two years older than she. For as long as she could remember, he was almost like a guardian angel. He even saved her life when she was six and fell into an irrigation ditch.

One warm fall evening Greta and Kurt relaxed comfortably on the patio of their home. A beautiful sunset painted the whole dome of the sky. Kurt shifted positions with a painful grunt.

"What's bothering you?" asked Greta.

"Sore spots from today's scrimmage," Kurt answered.

Greta looked thoughtfully at the sunset. Then she sat up and faced her brother. "Will you help me do something?" she asked brightly.

"Probably," he smiled.

She gulped a big breath. "Help me to get Mario to notice me!" she said quickly.

Kurt smiled. "You're both sophomores. You have classes together. You get him to notice you."

With a scowl of disappointment on her face, Greta leaned toward him. "Hey, don't be like that. You two are the stars of the football team. You're a senior and he looks up to you. If you pointed me out or something...."

After the game that Friday night, Greta sat in Kurt's pickup truck near the door from the locker room, waiting for her brother. She watched the four sophomore cheerleaders still jumping and laughing. Everyone was happy with the night's victory. Greta was especially proud of Kurt's performance.

Just as she thought, the cheerleaders were waiting for Mario. They crowded around him as he walked into the parking lot. He hugged two of them, one in each arm. Then they went off together, laughing. Greta was still pouting silently when Kurt slid into the truck.

After breakfast Saturday, Kurt went out to wash the family car. Greta went out to join him. She told him about the cheerleaders as they wiped the car. "Mario's not going to notice me unless you help me," she pleaded with her brother.

Kurt held up his hands. "Listen, I'm not playing matchmaker," he said firmly.

But one day that week, Mario and Kurt sat back-to-back in front of the two rows of lockers. Their conversation drifted from practice to Friday's opponent to a problem on one play.

Kurt moved to another subject. "You doing anything tonight?" he asked Mario.

"Nope. Probably go to bed early."

"How about a short double?"

"Did you have anything special in mind?" Mario asked.

"Nothing special," replied Kurt. "I want to be in early. How about an ice cream cone after dinner?"

"I'd like to, but I don't know who I'd ask," Mario repeated.

"Ask my little sister," offered Kurt. "I warn you, though: She won't settle for less than a sundae."

Later the four of them crowded into the cab of Kurt's pickup and went to the ice cream parlor. Greta had her sundae.

After that night, Mario started noticing Greta. That Friday, he talked to her twice. In math, where the teacher used no seating chart, he sat next to her. When she helped him with one of the homework problems, he patted a thank you on the top of her head. Before school, he talked to her in the hall.

Mario was noticing her; no question about that. Unfortunately, he was still noticing a lot of other girls. She was unhappy about that. When she complained to Kurt, he laughed at her. "I got him to notice you. Now it's your game!" Greta watched the next football game with two of her girl friends. Kurt and Mario combined to make the winning plays. One girl's dad had attended the game with them; he took them all home when it was over.

The next day Greta bubbled as she talked to Kurt about the game and how well he had played. When she began praising Mario, her excitement went even higher. "Wasn't he great?" she pleaded. "Oh, I think I love him!"

Kurt's big arm circled her tight. "Just stay friendly," he said softly. "Be helpful, be pleasant, but don't get pushy. He doesn't want a steady."

Sunday Mario asked Greta to go to a movie with him. Greta had a great time. She floated all week.

The following Friday at the last football game of the season,

Greta found out that Mario had asked someone else to go to the special Halloween movie. When she got home, she found a note. Her parents had gone out to play bridge. She knew she could not sleep so she sat up waiting for Kurt to come home.

Taking Time

1) Is Kurt helpful to Greta? In what ways?

2) Should Kurt do more to bring Greta and Mario together? Why or why not?

3) Should an older brother or sister always be expected to help a younger one? Why?

4) Is Greta doing enough to help herself? Explain.

5) Can Kurt (or any older brother or sister) do too much helping? Explain.

Putting Yourself in the Story

If you were Kurt, what would you do next?

In the Game Room

Randy and Bruce transferred into Lakeview High School on the same day in early December. That coincidence brought them together and they became friends even though they didn't have much in common. Randy was serious and hardworking while Bruce was easygoing and less responsible.

Randy and Bruce were in four of the same classes. They spent a lot of time together both in school and after. At the beginning of Christmas break, they went to the mall.

"You know, I'm beginning to like you," Bruce joked.

"Well, I guess you're not such bad company," Randy added.

They came to a store called The Game Room. Inside were every kind of video game and two long rows of pool tables.

"Play you a game of eight ball!" Bruce challenged.

Except for Christmas Eve and Christmas Day, Randy spent every evening of the vacation playing pool at The Game Room with Bruce. As they walked home, Randy said, "All this pool is getting boring."

"It's not boring, Randy. Don't you have fun?"

"Not really," replied Randy. "I feel guilty about just wasting so much time."

The day after New Year's Bruce went to stay overnight at Randy's. Randy had not gone to play pool for a week. Bruce, however, had gone by himself every night. After dinner with Randy's family, the boys spent the night watching TV.

"Aren't you going to play pool anymore?" asked Bruce.

"Oh, sure," Randy responded. "But not every night. We'll have homework again beginning tomorrow."

Two weeks later Randy met Bruce after school. They hadn't done anything together except go to class for the past two weeks.

"Listen, why don't we go play pool tonight?" Bruce suggested.

"Maybe," replied Randy. "I'll check and call you."

They played for almost three hours before Randy decided he had had enough. Bruce was getting better and better. He won every game.

"You need more practice," he goaded Randy.

"Oh, yeah?" Randy vetoed. "Well, you practice too much."
Bruce answered with a mocking laugh.

"I'm serious," Randy persisted. "Your grades are slipping. You better start hitting the books."

Bruce invited Randy to play pool with him again the next weekend. "Sorry, Bruce," Randy replied. "I can't do it. We have homework and I need all the time I can find."

Early in February Randy and Bruce ate lunch together. Bruce rather proudly told Randy that he had started shooting pool with some of the men for money.

"You mean you're gambling," Randy scolded.

"I guess you could call it that," agreed Bruce.

"Where are you getting the money?"

"An only kid gets a pretty good allowance," Bruce explained.

One day at the end of February, Randy nudged Bruce awake three times in their social studies class. On the way to their next class Bruce explained that he had played very late the night before. He was winning much more than losing and the older men kept him there to try to get their money back. Randy scowled at his friend.

"Bruce, you're ruining your life with that pool cue!"

Taking Time

1) How has Randy tried to help Bruce?

2) What are some other ways Randy might use to help Bruce?

3) Bruce is caught up in habitual play on the billiard tables. How could you help someone overcome a habit?

4) Bruce is now flirting with gambling, which is an addictive activity. Should Randy try to help him? How?

5) No one becomes addicted to any habit in a day or two. What does this tell us about any helping effort? Explain.

Putting Yourself in the Story

If you were Randy, what would you do next?

Everyone Will Know

The summer vacation was in full swing. School had closed the first week in June. Most of the ninth-graders newly graduated from Carroll Junior High were too young to get any of the jobs that were available. A few of them were babysitting or cutting grass. City recreation programs provided some activities, but the summer was already getting boring.

Neal and Kay were doubling with Mark and Bridget at the bowling alley. Kay was a quick person with a string of clever remarks. She frequently aimed humorous barbs at some individual—including herself. Bridget was the only one with a regular job. She worked every night except Monday and Tuesday at an ice cream parlor.

"Hey, Bridget, can't you trade with somebody on Fridays?" Neal asked. "Then you could play volleyball with us."

"Sorry. Everyone wants Fridays off, and I have the least seniority," replied Bridget.

"Dull! Dull! Dull!" chanted Kay.

"Yeah, but oh, so rich," Mark countered.

That Friday was the opening night of the junior volleyball league, which involved 16 teams of eight players from around the city. The schedule lasted seven Fridays; each team played two matches each night. Three squads of Carroll grads relaxed on one of those large grassy areas where teams waited to play.

"Hey, people!" Kay called out. "We have picked our team name. We're the Lawn Mowers and we're going to cut you down." A chorus of boos greeted her.

The next Friday it was almost ten o'clock when the games were over. Most of the Carroll people were hanging around, talking and laughing.

"Let's do something exciting," suggested Neal.

"It's getting late. I have to be home soon," someone added.

"How about tomorrow?" Kay asked. "Let's go skinny-dipping!" The only response was a few giggles. "Oh, come on," she tried again.

Some people left. Others stayed to laugh and talk about the

suggestion. After a little while, only eight remained. "Are you guys game?" Neal inquired. "Say something."

"If Kit wants to go, I'll go with her," Barney volunteered.

"I'll go and I won't let Leo chicken out," Nina snickered.

"We'll go," reported Lola, whose steady was Roger, a high school senior.

"OK!" Kay declared, clapping her hands. "Roger can you drive your truck?"

"Yeah!"

"Okay," Kay declared. "One last thing. Bring a picnic lunch— we'll tell everyone we're going on a picnic!"

By ten o'clock the next morning they were on their way. Nina rode up front with Lola and Roger. The others rode in the back of the truck under the camper shell. As usual, Kay was entertaining them with a flow of comments about everything, including their destination. Kit, who was crammed into the corner next to Barney, was absolutely quiet. "You all right?" he asked, leaning close to her.

"I've never done anything like this."

Barney's voice was kind as he spoke softly to her. "You probably can't back out now. They'd never let you. Just stay with the group. This kind of party you're safest when everybody can see you."

He squeezed her hand and smiled. She squeezed and smiled back. Barney tried to quiet her fears with some information. "Nobody goes to Hidden Lake right now. They just restocked it with little three-inch fish in May. It'll be a long time before fishermen go near the place."

There was no volleyball scheduled the next Friday because it was the Fourth of July weekend. Neal stopped to see Mark. "We had a great time at the lake," he reported. "Why didn't you go?"

"Bridget was working. Even if she wasn't, she wouldn't do that and I really wonder what you proved," Mark responded.

"So whatever," shrugged Neal. "Kay and I went all out. We sneaked away into the forest by ourselves. Went all the way."

"Is she on the pill or something?" Mark asked.

"Nope. She thought it was the right time of the month."

Mark frowned and shook his head. "That's really stupid gambling," he commented.

Toward the end of summer, Kay asked Kit to meet her near

the volleyball courts in the park. Kay was a little late. "What's up?" Kit asked her.

"I needed to talk to you," Kay replied. "I wanted it to be private. But everyone will know soon enough."

Kit just looked at her and waited.

"Remember when Neal and I sneaked off at Hidden Lake? Well, I'm pregnant."

"Are you sure?"

"Of course. Mom took me to the doctor. My dad called Neal's parents. They all want me to have an abortion. I won't do it. I threatened suicide if they make me—told them I'd join the baby. Neither Neal nor I can imagine getting married." Kay wiped her eyes.

"I had to talk to someone, Kit. You're the only one who was there that would understand," Kay said.

A few days later Kit met with Bridget, Mark and Barney. She told them exactly what she knew about Kay.

"Listen, she needs help. She's going to need all kinds of support when school starts. Her dad is awfully angry with her, but I talked to her mom. I think we can win her mom over, and maybe later her dad. When the baby comes, she'll need help deciding whether or not to keep it and ways to support it and still finish school if she does. Her suicide threat really scares me. She will have an awful problem if she should lose the baby," Kit stopped to catch her breath. "How can we help her?"

Taking Time

1) What might Neal have done to help Kay? What should he do to help her now?

2) In what ways was Mark helpful and to whom?

3) In what ways was Barney helpful and to whom?

4) How does Kit indicate that she sees helping Kay as a long-time effort?

5) What can Kit, Bridget, Mark and Barney do to help Kay during the next months? The next year?

Putting Yourself in the Story

If you were one of Kay's classmates and wanted to help her, what could you do?

Teddy Bear

Leon was the largest boy in the freshman class. His art teacher once described him as having the strength of an elephant and the disposition of a teddy bear.

Early in the year Leon walked out of school with Larry. "It's a beautiful day!" Larry exclaimed. "Want to go for a walk?"

"Don't you have to get home?" Leon asked.

"My mom and dad are both lawyers. My sister takes care of my little brothers. No reason for me to go home," Larry laughed.

"My mom works, too," Leon explained. "My dad got killed. He was a police officer."

Larry and Leon began to meet after school most days. One day they stopped at a sporting goods store to look at baseball gloves. As they left and turned along the sidewalk, Larry banged into one of three boys walking toward them.

"Hey, watch where you're going," Larry growled.

"You're the one who was gawking at the window," the other boy retorted.

That was all Larry needed. He charged the much larger boy but proved no match for his longer arms. After seeing Larry take a couple good punches, Leon stepped in.

"That's enough," he said firmly.

The tall boy dodged Larry. "I'll decide when he's had enough," he called to Leon.

Leon quickly pulled Larry aside and faced the other boy. "You want some, too?" he asked Leon.

As the boy swung his fist, Leon brushed it aside and knocked him flat with one punch. At that, the two other guys ran at Leon. He shoved one into the other, sending them both sprawling.

"The fight's over," Leon ordered.

Leon, towering over Larry, pushed him ahead. The three others let them go.

A week later, Leon stopped to see his mother at the supermarket where she worked. As usual, Larry walked along with him.

"Hi, Mom," Leon greeted her, giving her a quick kiss on the

cheek. "Can I buy a new drawing pad?"

He went to the art supply section to pick out the pad. As Leon and Larry left the store, Larry touched his friend's arm.

"Did you see that pile of candy bars? It'd be easy to just take a couple of those!"

Leon shook his head. "That would be stupid," he said. "I know a better way."

"What's that?" asked Larry.

"Tomorrow I'll show you," Leon promised.

"Where are we going?" Larry asked as they left school the next day.

Leon trudged along, his drawing pad under his arm, with a smile on his face. "Out to the truck stop," he answered.

Fifteen minutes later they were at the complex of diesel pumps and food shops. Leon went directly to the very small table in the corner of the cafe. "Now you'll see," he grinned at Larry.

He was already sketching something on his pad. As Larry watched, a face began to take form. Soon Leon had penciled an attractive caricature. He went over to the tall truck driver who sat at the counter drinking coffee.

"Yeah, whatcha want, kid?" the man asked.

Leon handed him the sketch.

"Hey, that's me!" the driver exclaimed.

"That's right," Leon agreed. "Want to buy it for your girl?"

"How much?"

"Oh, just a couple bucks."

The big man dug into his pocket and handed Leon three singles. Leon thanked him. As he and Larry left, Leon bought two candy bars and handed Larry one.

The next afternoon Larry sat in the barber shop watching Leon draw more caricatures. In two hours he sold three.

"Is mine ready?" asked a small white-haired man as he stepped from the chair.

Leon peeled the sheet from his pad and handed it to the man, who held it up for the barber to see. Both laughed at the distorted face and figure.

"My wife'll say the kid made me too handsome!" With that, the man handed Leon five dollars and left the shop.

"OK," said the barber, "you two have hung around here long

134

enough. Ain't you got homes?"

Leon flashed a big grin. "Nope," he replied. "Just a big box down by the tracks."

As he and Larry backed toward the door, Leon handed the pursuing barber a caricature complete with clippers and chair. Two drawings already hung on the wall of the shop.

Outside on the street, Larry faced his friend. "Leon, what do you do with all the money you make with your drawings?"

Leon shrugged. "Just give Mom most of it. She's having a hard time since my dad got killed."

Taking Time

1) What are some ways that Leon helps his mother?

2) Is the help Leon gives his mother a one-time effort? Explain.

3) How does Leon help his friend Larry?

4) Does Leon use his talents to help others? Explain.

5) Would you say that Larry is a helpful person? Why or why not?

6) Would you say that people relate to Leon in a helpful manner? Explain.

Putting Yourself in the Story

If you were Larry, what would you learn from Leon?